"It took me more than thirty years to write my first book. I wish I had read Tom's first and realized I had a choice to write one a lot earlier than that. Choose to read this book and then choose to follow the incredibly helpful advice inside to see just how powerful a choice can be."

—Jon Acuff, *New York Times* bestselling author of
Finish: Give Yourself the Gift of Done

"The Ziglar family name has been synonymous with winning for decades. Tom Ziglar brings a fresh approach and shows us how success is always a choice."

—Brian Buffini, Buffini & Company

"*Choose to Win* is written to assist each of us on our life's journey, beginning today with particularly uncommon clarity to motivate action where it's needed! Thanks, Tom, for immediately adding significant value to my net worth as an individual."

—Larry R. Carpenter, president/CEO, Carpenter Hotel Group, LLC

"A wise man once said that if you were to pull someone up you had better be on higher ground. Tom Ziglar writes a brilliant book from higher ground. It is authored with clarity, offered with confidence, and illustrated with competence. The concepts and missives outlined in the book bring the desire for choice to the edge of the page being read and then force the imagination of the reader to assume responsibility. That in my mind is the definition of wisdom from higher ground. You will be blessed for having read it and then blessed again when you apply the principles outlined within."

—Krish Dhanam, author and speaker

"*Choose to Win* is the perfect modern-day manual to not only learn how to transform your life, but to do it in a simple but highly effective manner. Engaging, inspiring, and full of incredible significance, this book is essential reading for anyone wanting to take their goals and legacy to the next level."

—Chris Ducker, bestselling author of *Rise of the Youpreneur*

"I believe that being an effective leader is a choice that starts with choosing the habits that will automatically produce the character qualities every leader must have. *Choose to Win* is the perfect book at the right time to help identify and put into practice the habits you need to become the best leader possible."

—Dina Dwyer-Owens, brand ambassador for
Neighborly; cochair, The Dwyer Group

"Tom has an amazing way of taking the complex and simplifying it. How does he do this? By asking questions, challenging questions. Questions that may be difficult to answer. Questions you've postponed asking yourself. And, once you've addressed those questions, Tom provides a guide to use to find the answers to build your personal legacy."

—Bryan Flanagan, flanagantraining.com

"Focusing on seven key areas of life—personal success, career advancement, physical health, family cohesiveness, mental wellness, financial independence, and spiritual well-being—*Choose to Win* offers a step-by-step guide to finding real success and building a lasting legacy. I've known Tom both personally and professionally and can assure you, he practices what he preaches."

—Jason Frenn, international speaker and bestselling author

"I read this book in one sitting from cover to cover, taking many notes in the process. I highly recommend you read *Choose to Win* at least twice. The first time for pure enjoyment. You want to savor every one of Tom's entertaining stories. For the second reading, I suggest you highlight all the great success principles and action tips to create the best version of you. You can make that choice today. This book is a powerful guide for creating a more successful, meaningful, and purposeful life."

—Gerhard Gschwandtner, CEO, SellingPower.com

"I have always loved Zig Ziglar's philosophy of *Be* the right person, *Do* the right things, so that you can *Have* all that life has to offer. Tom Ziglar's *Choose to Win* is the 'how to' action plan for Be, Do, and Have!"

—Kevin Harrington, original shark on *Shark Tank*;
inventor of the infomercial

"I read a lot of articles and books throughout the year. I have received actionable goals out of this book, more than any other I have read. I started putting to practice some of the principles Tom shared the very next day. When the mind and heart are working together, you can achieve anything. That is what Tom's book has accomplished, connects the mind and heart."

—Jimmy Hiller, Hiller Plumbing, Heating, Cooling and Electrical

"In *Choose to Win*, Tom Ziglar shares ways to achieve goals to become who we are designed to be and lead the reader through the Wheel of Life, using riveting personal stories and a hint of humor."

—Charles Ho, real estate and people investor, multi-family syndicator

"Filled with nuggets of gold. My favorite is that the fastest way to success is to replace bad habits with good ones."

—Guy Kawasaki, Chief Evangelist of Canva and
author of *Wise Guy: Lessons from a Life*

"And who wouldn't choose to win? But how to transform that sentiment into a strategy? And how to execute that strategy? For the answers to these two critical questions, we must all thank Tom Ziglar. This book takes the reader from desire to determination and from timidity to triumph. Win, indeed!"

—Rabbi Daniel Lapin, author of *Thou Shall Prosper*
and *Business Secrets from the Bible*

"In *Choose to Win*, Tom Ziglar reveals seven choices where by making tiny, incremental changes you can transform your life. This book has had a profound impact on my thinking."

—Ryan Levesque, #1 national bestselling author of *Choose.* and *Ask.*

"Developing a heightened awareness of our power to choose is absolutely essential. It is the very key to whether we grow and succeed or atrophy and fail. This is beautifully illustrated in *Choose to Win*."

—Greg McKeown, *New York Times* bestselling author
of *Essentialism: The Disciplined Pursuit of Less*

"We can still choose character, honesty, love, and loyalty to put us on the path to true winning. These are timeless principles that honor the Ziglar name and legacy."

—Dan Miller, *New York Times* bestselling author
of *48 Days to the Work You Love*

"You will love the book, and you will love the man. Over the past seven years, I've traveled the world with Tom Ziglar. I've been deeply involved with his business and his family. You won't find a person who is more sincere about helping you than Tom. This book will help you choose the habits that will help you win in life!"

—Howard Partridge, international business coach

"Do you want to live a life of happiness, good health, strong relationships, success, and prosperity? Of course you do! We all want to be winners in life, and as Tom Ziglar so beautifully explains, living to win is a choice. *Choose to Win* is a practical book with time-tested principles that will radically change your life. Don't just read this book—highlight it, devour it, apply it, and choose to be a winner in life!"

—Michelle Prince, author, speaker, and publisher

"I was blessed to call Zig Ziglar my friend, and I'm blessed to say the same about his son, Tom. Over the years, I've watched him grow into a gifted leader, so I know the principles found in *Choose to Win* can change your life. This is a must-read book for anyone looking to shake things up and actually take ownership of their future."

—Dave Ramsey, bestselling author and nationally
syndicated radio show host

"*Choose to Win* is what you'd expect from the Ziglar name in 2019: simple, downhome, actionable positivity based in character, integrity, and the Ziglar Qualities of Success, illustrated with stories from Tom's life, family, and renowned friends. From basics like sleep, diet, and exercise to periodically a nugget that you didn't realize you were missing and hits the spot, Tom shares what to do to create your legacy."

—Joshua Spodek, PhD, MBA, professor of leadership
and author of *Leadership Step by Step*

"*Choose to Win* is a must-read for anyone and everyone! Tom Ziglar has truly delivered a masterpiece with this book!"

—Logan Stout, entrepreneur, author, speaker, founder
and CEO, IDLife and Dallas Patriots, Inc.

CHOOSE
TO WIN

TRANSFORM YOUR LIFE, ONE
SIMPLE CHOICE AT A TIME

TOM ZIGLAR

NELSON
BOOKS

An Imprint of Thomas Nelson

Published in Nashville, Tennessee, by Nelson Books, an imprint of Thomas Nelson. Nelson Books and Thomas Nelson are registered trademarks of HarperCollins Christian Publishing, Inc.

Published in association with the literary agency of Literary Management Group, LLC.

Thomas Nelson titles may be purchased in bulk for educational, business, fund-raising, or sales promotional use. For information, please e-mail SpecialMarkets@ThomasNelson.com.

Any Internet addresses, phone numbers, or company or product information printed in this book are offered as a resource and are not intended in any way to be or to imply an endorsement by Thomas Nelson, nor does Thomas Nelson vouch for the existence, content, or services of these sites, phone numbers, companies, or products beyond the life of this book.

Scripture quotations are taken from the ESV® Bible (The Holy Bible, English Standard Version®), copyright © 2001 by Crossway, a publishing ministry of Good News Publishers. Used by permission. All rights reserved.

ISBN 978-1-4002-0952-1 (eBook)
ISBN 978-1-4002-0954-5 (HC)
ISBN 978-1-4002-1295-8 (IE)
ISBN 978-1-4002-0953-8 (TP)

Library of Congress Control Number: 2018955685

21 22 23 24 25 LSC 10 9 8 7 6 5 4 3 2 1

What will your last words to those you love be?

I am dedicating this book to Mom and Dad, Jean and Zig Ziglar. They both provided me everything. Their words, actions, and faith in God were always loud and clear and they echo in my heart. They showed me by example how to Choose to Win.

If I could have had anyone write the foreword to this book, it would have been Mom and Dad. And then I realized—they did.

My dad's last written words to me were, "For my son who I love and am very proud and grateful for. Romans 8:28"

For My Son who I love
and am Very proud and grateful for
Rom 8-28

Dad was struggling with Alzheimer's, and you can tell that he struggled to write the sentence—so much so that you can see his heart in the writing.

Mom's last words to me were in the hospital, forty-eight hours before she passed into eternity. As I was leaving, she motioned for me to come over to her. I leaned over, and she grabbed my neck and whispered in my ear, "I am soooooooo, so proud of you, and I love you sooooooo, so much."

Mom and Dad left a legacy that will ripple through eternity. It was by design, based on the intentional choices they made.

You can leave a legacy by design as well.

So, I will ask you again—What will your last words be?

CONTENTS

SECTION I: IT STARTS WITH *WHY*

SECTION II: THE 7 CHOICES PLAN

SECTION III: WHEN DO I START?

CONTENTS

Section I

IT STARTS WITH *WHY*

As a speaker and executive coach, perhaps the most common question I hear is: "Tom, I am not sure if what I am doing right now in my life is the right thing. Can you give me some advice on my *what*?" They will then tell me about their current frustrations with their job, career, business, or direction in life. I simply respond with a question: "Why are you doing your *what*?" Nine times out of ten, the person shrugs and gives a rambling answer.

It's important to clarify your *why*. When you do, it opens doors to your *what* and transforms *how* you do everything. Planning becomes fun, and going the extra mile in everything you do is now just how you live life.

Anybody can have an incredible day, or week, or even a month, but to make your *how* extraordinary over your entire life, you need a big *why*. Good news—discovering your *why* is a choice! And when your *why* becomes clear, the *how* transforms and multiple doors of *what* open up for you.

Chapter 1
....

WHAT IS YOUR *WHY*?

Define Success, Significance, and Legacy

What's your *why*?

I had just finished speaking at an event when a young man approached me. "I believe what you said is true about goals and finding your *why*, but I know me, and I know that I will start working on my goals for about three days and then I will get distracted. How can I stay focused on doing what I know I need to do?"

As we began to talk, I asked him questions. I learned that he had four kids under the age of six, was close to thirty years old, had a very good job, and was a high performer. He wanted to take control of his future without being at the mercy of his employer. He wanted balanced success in all areas of life.

Since we didn't have much time to talk, he pressed me again for an answer. "How do I get started so that I can consistently work on my goals?"

"Are you serious enough to start with committing fifteen minutes a day to building the life you want?" I asked.

"Yes," he said.

"Great! Here is what I recommend. You need to develop a couple of foundational habits that will impact everything else you do. I would like for you to start every day by doing these three things. Number one, set aside the first fifteen minutes of the day. Can you do that?"

"Yes," he said.

"Number two, you need to change your mind-set and how you see yourself. We have created Ziglar self-talk cards, found on page 222, that I would like you to read out loud to yourself while you are looking in the mirror. You have all the qualities of success—like discipline, integrity, loyalty, and about thirty-five others—already inside of you; they just need to be recognized, claimed, and developed. This daily practice will change the way you see yourself, and this will change how you behave, which will get you the results you want. Can you commit to reading the card each morning? It takes about three minutes."

"Yes, I can commit to that," he said.

"Number three, I would like you to invest about twelve minutes reviewing the top four goals you are currently working on and then plan and prioritize your day. This is the time you reconfirm your big priorities and goals and commit to doing the things that will create the life you want. Can you do this as well?"

"Yes," he said, "but I know me. I'll start this, and after about three days, I'll go back to my habits of staying up late watching TV or playing video games. How do I stay focused?"

This guy was saying aloud what almost everyone thinks:

I know I should, but ...
That plan will work, if only I weren't so ...
It surely would be nice, but ....

You get the picture.

I asked, "If you did these things every day, would it pay off for you?"

"Yes, absolutely," he said.

"How?"

"Oh, it would change my life. I have big things I want to do, and know I can do—"

"Great!" I said. "What do you mean by change your life? Would it mean more money for you?"

"Yes, it would," he said.

"More than $10,000 over the year?"

"Yes, easily," he said.

"That sounds well worth getting up fifteen minutes earlier each day. What do you think?"

"Yes, it does. But I *know me*. After about three days I will stop."

"I have a proposal for you that I believe will keep you on track. It takes about sixty-six days to form a new good habit and keep it. I propose that you write me a check for $10,000 today, and then for the next sixty-six days you start off each day as I suggested and daily send me a text message telling me you have done the fifteen-minute prep time. At the end of the sixty-six days, if you have done this every single day, I will return your $10,000. If you miss even one day, I get to keep it. Do you think you would do it then?"

"Yes. I know I would. No question about it," he said.

"Why would you do it in the second scenario when you told me the first scenario would make you $10,000 as well?"

"Fear of loss, I guess."

I love honest people.

Here is the point: it's a choice!

Creating the life you want is a choice. The young man was in his comfort zone. He wasn't feeling much pain. Giving me the $10,000 would have raised his pain level enough to motivate him to wake up fifteen minutes earlier every day. Isn't this the way most people live? Coasting along in the slow lane of mediocrity. The only time they change lanes is to avoid an accident or after they have had an accident.

Think about it.

People get serious about a budget when the repo man shows up to take their car.

People get serious about working on their health as they are being wheeled into emergency surgery to get a heart stent.

People get serious about working on their marriage when their spouse says they are filing for divorce.

Good news. It doesn't have to be this way. We all need what the young man was missing. A clearly defined *why*. A dream so big and so compelling it draws us like a magnet.

What is your *why*? What is your dream?

Don't have one yet? That's okay. Get ready. This book is going to take you on a journey from survival to stability, to success, to significance, and finally, to legacy.

Maybe you have a big *why* and big dreams, but you don't know how to achieve them. Perfect. You are in the right place.

SURVIVAL

When you don't know where you are going, any direction will do.

Survival mode is when you don't know who you are and you don't know the person you want to become. Your goal is simply to make it through another day and pay the bills. People in survival mode will take almost any job that meets their basic needs, regardless of whether they are passionate about it, because they don't believe they have a choice. If others are telling you what you should do and you are just going along with it, you are likely in survival mode.

STABILITY

"I know what I want."

Stability is when you know what you want and who you want to become. You are no longer guided by the winds of life; instead, you are motivated by the desire to become the person God created you to become. You may not know exactly where life is taking you, but you know the direction you are headed, and you are excited about growing as a person. Each opportunity you accept is based on understanding what you want out of life and not just on the opinion of others.

SUCCESS

What is your definition of success?

Unfortunately, too many people have the wrong definition. Success is more than money, or fame, or nice stuff. I heard a radio advertisement for a law firm specializing in child custody cases. It addressed the number of men who had traded their health and family relationships for career success, and even though they now had a lot of money, they couldn't buy back their health or families. If you are going to live to win, you need balanced success in all seven areas of life: mental, spiritual, physical, family, financial, personal, and career. I learned this concept from my father, Zig Ziglar, at an early age, and I grew up watching him work daily on each of these areas.

> "Success is the maximum utilization of the abilities that God gave you."
> —ZIG ZIGLAR

One of the expectations we set for ourselves is measuring our success against others' accomplishments; but it doesn't take long for us to realize that some people have more than we do in certain areas and other people have less. I love a great success story, and success stories often inspire me, but none of them define my potential for success.

Those with the right success mind-set understand that the way we see our future is much more important than our past, what others are doing, or our current circumstances.

For more than forty years of my life, I had the privilege of watching my father speak countless times to thousands of people. Dad would mesmerize the crowd, and they would laugh and learn and believe in themselves. How did he do it? He gave them hope!

My dad regularly asked his audiences to do two things. First, he said, "Raise your hand if there is anything you can do in your personal life, your business life, your family life, or your spiritual life in the next seven days that would make your life *worse*."

After the crowd heard the first request, they would murmur in surprise, shocked that the most optimistic and positive man on the planet would ask the audience to consider such a negative question. Of course you can do something that will make your life worse! You can cut off your finger, cuss out your boss—the list goes on and on.

Then he would make the second request: "Raise your hand if there is anything you can do in your personal life, your business life, your family life, or your spiritual life in the next seven days that would make your life *better*."

After this request, I would scan the audience and see thousands of hands go up! Of course you can make your life better. You can send an "I love you" text to a family member or a close friend. You can exercise, eat a healthy meal, get more than seven hours of sleep—the list goes on and on.

Here is the point in the success mind-set. Hope is born when you understand this: *you have the power to make things better or worse, and the choice is yours.*

The choice is yours. *Choose to Win: Transform Your Life One Simple Choice at a Time* is about convincing you to use the power you already have to create the life you really want.

"But *my* situation is unique," you may be saying. "Maybe you have the power, or others have the power, but not me. You don't understand what I have been through."

It's true. A success mind-set is simple to describe, but it's not easy to do. It takes some work. First, you have to believe that you have the power to make things better. Then you have to take action and change the way you see your past.

Reclaiming the Past

When I do executive coaching, I love to use the question "Are you kidding me?" in a strong voice. I learned this concept from one of my mentors, Dale Dodson. Dale is an extremely successful businessman and the chairman of our board, but like everyone I know, he has faced major challenges and setbacks. He often asked me tough business questions, and I would give him a reason why we couldn't do something, and he would say, "Are you kidding me?" And then he would explain that often the reason I wasn't going to do something was the very reason I should.

A number of years ago, I had a coaching call with an individual who was struggling with where he was in life. He had lost all confidence in his ability to do his job. He and his wife were Realtors, and when the housing bubble burst in 2008, their combined income went from more than $400,000 to under $70,000. Financially, they lost almost everything, their marriage suffered, and they almost split up. When I spoke to him, their marriage was stable, but the housing market still had not recovered and his career was at rock bottom.

Here is how our conversation went:

"Tom, I just don't think I can keep doing real estate. I mean, who would want me? We've lost everything. Why would anyone want to do business with me?"

"Are you kidding me?" I answered.

Silence on the other end of the phone.

11

"Are you *kidding me?*"

"Tom, I don't understand. Why are you asking me that?"

"Let me ask you another question. Since the real estate bubble burst, do you know more or less about how to do a real estate deal?"

"Oh, I know far more than I did before. I've had to get creative. The easy deals are gone," he answered.

"What percentage of the transactions in the market right now involve people in desperate situations?" I asked.

"Most of them," he said.

"So, you are telling me that you know far more about real estate now than you did a few years ago, and the majority of the people in the market right now are experiencing the same pain you have experienced. They are scared and not sure how to make things work."

"Yes, that is correct," he answered.

"Are you kidding me?" I asked again.

"What do you mean by that question, Tom?"

"You just told me that you know more about real estate today than at any time in your life, and that you have experienced personally the pain and fear of very tough circumstances, and that most of your clients and potential clients are in the exact same boat. The way I see it, you are perfectly positioned to help more people than you have ever helped before. Based on what I know about you, I believe you can help your clients better than anyone else in your market because you live your life with integrity and you have struggled and won the battle for your marriage. The market needs you, your skills, and your experience, now more than ever."

"Okay. Wow! I wasn't looking at it that way," he responded.

We then talked about what he could do to grow his business, focusing on solutions and not on the problem. He had already acknowledged the problem, which was good, but dwelling on the problem didn't solve it. Focusing on solutions and then taking action are the key ingredients to success.

Nothing in his life had changed, but his view of his circumstances had. Before we talked, his circumstances were the reason he should quit. After I spoke to him, his circumstances became the fuel for why he should continue.

About a week after our phone call, I got a seven-page, single-spaced email from him describing a new client. He had been digging into his leads and calling homeowners whose houses had recently been delisted because they were not selling. One woman's response about listing her house was filled with hopelessness because, she said, the market was bad, she was going through a divorce, and her soon-to-be ex-husband wouldn't agree to the sale anyway.

He told her about his experience in the marketplace and a little about his personal family struggles and said he would love to help her. With nothing to lose, she agreed to let him try and said, "You need to get my soon-to-be ex-husband on board."

He described going on a cold call to meet her husband, who was living at a friend's house. He explained that he was trying to help and shared a little bit about his own circumstances. The man's shoulders slumped and he agreed it was time to move on and then signed the paperwork.

He got the deal!

What about you? Are you going to change your mind-set regarding your past? Our Realtor friend got the deal *because* of what he had been through, and this happened only because he chose to see his past as the reason for moving forward, not the reason to quit.

I share these stories to give you hope and encouragement. No matter where you are in your life, no matter your past mistakes or circumstances beyond your control, *you can make things better or worse right now, and the choice is yours.* Your past is important because it uniquely positions you to help other people in the future in ways that no one else can. By changing your mind-set regarding your past, you start building your future success today.

> ....
> "Success is the
> progressive
> realization of a worthy
> goal or ideal."
> —EARL NIGHTINGALE
> ....

True success is spiritual, and it often must be purified in the furnace before it grows into significance.

Success can be described as what we achieve for ourselves. One of the by-products of success is happiness. If you are looking for another *why*, then you just found a big one right here. I believe we all want to be happy. Changing your mind-set about success and making daily progress toward a worthy goal or ideal will produce happiness in your life.

Do you want to be happy? Pursue the right kind of success!

SIGNIFICANCE

Without even realizing it, our Realtor friend moved from success to the furnace to significance.

Significance is on a completely different level. Success and happiness are circumstantial, based largely on cause and effect. This is good, but it also can be temporary and dependent upon the next thing you do, and the next thing you do, and the next thing you do.

The *why* of significance is simple. Happiness is fantastic, but there is something even better: joy. Joy is the by-product of significance.

> ....
> Significance is when you help others be, do,
> or have more than they thought possible.
> ....

Pure joy comes when you help other people. Joy is the fruit of your labor when your words and your actions allow others to release the potential inside of them. This is why being a parent can be so fulfilling and joyful and so frustrating and overwhelming at the same time. Our hearts want the best for our children, and there is no greater joy in life than helping your own children unleash their potential. Joy is not dependent on circumstances or how you are personally doing. You can experience joy at any moment.

The *why* of success is good. The *why* of significance is better than good!

Moving from success to significance often requires spending time in the furnace—and none of us enjoy being in the furnace. How many times in your own life have you given or received advice that was meaningful and helpful only because the advice was purified in the furnace of life? The Realtor couldn't have helped the way he did without having been in the furnace, and the furnace set him up for significance. Are you in the furnace right now? Change your mind-set, knowing the time in the furnace is preparing you for significance.

I was discussing the furnace of life concept with DeWayne Owens. DeWayne is a longtime friend, a pastor, and the chaplain of our Ziglar Legacy Certified Trainers. We were talking about the story of Job from the Bible. Job had everything you could have in life. He was successful by all accounts. He then lost all his possessions, his friends, even his children. He was truly in the furnace. DeWayne pointed out something to me that really hit home. God restored everything to Job twofold, and then something amazing happened (Job 42:15). Job went counterculture. Job had three daughters, and he gave them an inheritance, breaking the social rules and customs of his time when only sons were recognized in this way. Why did he do that? Could it be that the furnace helped him understand what it meant to have less than nothing so that when he was restored, he had the compassion to bless all his children?

"I Am Glad This Happened to You"

Our company was blessed to have had Amy Jones on our team for a number of years. She was an amazing young speaker and author who passed away several years ago. I will never forget her furnace story, and how her mind-set totally shifted when she understood how the furnace positioned her to help others.

Amy had been married for about ten years when one day her husband disappeared. No note. No hint that he was leaving. Nothing. The fear, worry, chaos, and uncertainty were overwhelming. Had he been murdered or injured, or was he mentally ill? No one knew.

Amy filed missing-person reports with the police and to be able to do anything—like sell her car or her house—she filled out numerous legal documents. It was about a year before she knew if her husband was alive. It turns out he had had a complete mental breakdown and was living as a homeless person two thousand miles away. During this time she was befriended by a woman where she worked who took her in, supported her emotionally, and even invited her to family gatherings. This meant everything to Amy.

This kind lady offered to help Amy in any way she could. One day Amy asked if the lady would attend church with her and just sit by her for support. The lady told Amy that she and her family would go with her, not because they believed in God (they didn't), but because they wanted to support Amy. Over time, they started going regularly with Amy to church, and, as a result, the entire family became Christians. Amy shared with me that months after this happened she was having a really bad day and she started complaining to the lady and asking, "Why did this have to happen to me? Why me?"

Amy told me how the lady responded. "Amy," she said, "I know this might be hard for you to hear, but I am glad this happened to you. I wouldn't know God, and neither would my family, if it weren't for this situation."

Suddenly, the furnace had meaning and purpose for Amy, and she lived out the rest of her life knowing that her furnace ended up blessing her friend and many others. Amy's purpose moved from success to significance with this realization.

Hope. Success. Significance.

And legacy.

What will your legacy be?

Building an intentional legacy gives meaning and purpose to your life.

LEGACY

....

Success and significance are stepping-stones
on the way to legacy.

....

This is the biggest *why* of all: legacy. Legacy is eternal. Your legacy will ripple through eternity. You can stumble on success (at least the world's definition of success), but significance and the right kind of legacy are intentional. Do you want to be happy? Do you want a life filled with joy? Do you want your life to have meaning and purpose? Then make legacy your goal!

Whenever I speak, I always ask the audience: "Please raise your hand if you would like to leave a legacy." It doesn't matter if I am in Poland, Singapore, Holland, or Papua New Guinea, 100 percent of the hands go up! How about you? Do you want to leave a legacy? I have news for you. You are going to leave a legacy. The only question is, will it be by design or by chance?

....

Legacy is teaching and transferring the habits
that build character, integrity, and wisdom,
which will ripple through eternity.

....

Read that quote again. It's big. The choices you make today. What you do today. The decisions you make today. These will all ripple through eternity.

Legacy is much more than inheritance. I was having lunch one day with my good friend Bill Porter and he was sharing with me a client's challenge. His client owned more than twenty oil wells, and he was working with an estate planner on how to leave the oil wells to his adult children. His client's biggest concern was how to give his kids one oil well a year so that they wouldn't blow the money all at once and would always have a safety net. I told Bill that, yes, his client was leaving a big inheritance, but until and unless he transferred the habits that build character, integrity, and wisdom to his children, his legacy was uncertain.

....

Inheritance is physical; legacy is spiritual.

....

After you die, the inheritance you leave gets divided either according to your will or to the laws of the land if you had no will. The physical assets are distributed after any debts of the estate are paid. These physical assets are transferred to the designated recipients. Legacy is much bigger and much broader than inheritance because it is spiritual.

Legacy is the reputation, character, integrity, and wisdom that are successfully transferred.

Legacy is not money; it's living a life that creates money as a by-product of a life well lived.

Legacy is about transferring habits that build great relationships with family, friends, coworkers, customers, and God.

Have you ever noticed someone with a bad attitude? I am not talking about someone who is having a bad day, but rather a pattern of behavior that shows up in that person's attitude. Take, for example, the attitude of entitlement.

....

Attitude is a reflection of character, and
character is a reflection of habit.

....

Someone with an entitled attitude has a character flaw created through bad habits. The opposite attitude of entitlement is gratitude. Gratitude is simply focusing on all the things we do have. The habit of gratitude is built by daily recognizing all the small and big things that make our life better. By giving thanks in this way, we train our brains to look for more things to be grateful for.

People with high levels of gratitude are happier and more generous and more pleasant to be around. They also spend less time in prison than those who feel entitled! Yes, you read that right. People who feel entitled will justify taking things that do not belong to them because "It's not fair. They have something I don't, and the only way I am going to get it is to take it." People who are filled with gratitude are the opposite because they realize they have so much, and they are eager to share what they have with others.

The friction between entitlement and gratitude is just one example of what you are creating in your legacy. You are going to influence those around you, and this influence creates your legacy. Here is the good news: how you influence others is your choice!

What if your legacy became your *why*? Only you can leave your legacy. You are unique, created by God with gifts and talents only you have. Only you have lived your life and been through your furnaces.

No one else has your experiences. No one else can leave your legacy. Only you can leave your legacy.

The legacy you leave will ripple through eternity. Will the ripples you create propel those you love to their own lives of success, significance, and legacy? Are you willing to leave something this big to chance? Make legacy your *why* and take daily steps toward it, and you will experience greater success and significance as part of the journey.

"You were designed for accomplishment, engineered for success, and endowed with the seeds of greatness."

—ZIG ZIGLAR

What do you want to be known for? What reputation do you want your family to have? When people talk about you and your family when you're not around, what do you want them to say? Answering these questions is the first step you need to take as you start creating your intentional legacy.

I want you to start thinking of key words and phrases that you want you and your family to be known for. The Ziglar family is known by several words and phrases. *Hope* and *encouragement* come to my mind first. I can remember as a little boy asking Dad what he did. He always said, "Son, we sell hope. People need hope and encouragement now more than ever. If we help people in this way, it will give them the courage to step out and try." In fact, Dad taught the Encouragers Sunday school class at our church for years, and if you ever heard him speak or listened to him on a recording, I know you will agree that he always left an audience with a big dose of hope and encouragement.

Two more words the Ziglar family is known for are *character* and *integrity*. This is our reputation as a brand. When people asked Dad what his number one reason for success was, he always answered "character and integrity." One of Dad's greatest habits he transferred to us was his habit of always doing the right thing, no matter how difficult it might be or how compelling the shortcut might look.

A few years before Dad passed away, I asked him what the number two reason for his success was, and he answered, "Persistent consistency." He then explained: "Consistency is when you have a worthwhile objective or goal and you work on it every day or as often as necessary. Persistence is when you always do a little bit extra while you are working consistently toward your worthwhile goal or objective." In a nutshell, Dad said his two keys to success were character and integrity and his work ethic (persistent consistency).

What are the words you want your family to be known for? *Love? Kindness? Courage? Generosity? Weirdness?* Yes, I said weirdness! Let me explain. I asked my good friends Betty and Charles Ho what words they wanted their family to be known for. One of the words Charles picked was *weird*. Smiling, I asked Charles why.

Charles said, "Simple. When we sit around the table discussing things with our family about what is going on in school and in life, it seems that as a family we all decide to do exactly the opposite of whatever everyone else is doing. Our daughter Elizabeth said, 'Dad, we are weird,' and that word *weird* became a badge of honor for our family. We figure if we are doing the opposite of the popular culture, we will do just fine!"

What are the words you want your family to be known for? The words that, if lived out, will ripple through eternity in all the right ways? Don't worry if you are not good at these words yet. These words are the future and the legacy you are going to create. Go ahead and write down these words on a piece of paper or in a journal.

How does it feel to claim the words you want your family to be known for? Later in the book I will go into detail about how you can make these words part of your family's DNA through simple choices that turn into habits that create legacy.

Right now I want you to dream a little bit with me.

Have you ever thought about your dream home? You might be in the time of life when you are just surviving, hoping to make it another week. That is okay. You can still dream, and dreams give you the inspiration and motivation you need to keep moving forward. You might already have a clearly defined dream home, and when you close your eyes you can clearly see it. Or you could be living in your dream home, and when you close your eyes you dream about your grandkids living in their dream homes! Wherever you are on the journey, join me for a second and think about your dream home.

Where is it located? In the mountains? On a beach? By a lake or on a family farm? It's your dream home, so you get to pick. Now fill in the details. I will use my dream home as an example. My dream home is in the mountains surrounded by trees. All you can hear is the sound of the trout stream running next to the house. The scent of pine needles is in the air. The three-story front of the house is facing the mountain peaks, and it has plenty of windows to take in the view. The wraparound porch always provides a place to find sunlight or shade and is perfect for a quiet cup of coffee during morning devotionals or for a family feast next to the grill. You can't see any of the neighbors' houses, but they are less than a five-minute walk away, and there are plenty of hiking trails and good places to fish within a short distance.

Sounds good, doesn't it? It gets better. I have plenty of bedrooms for my entire family and a ton of friends to visit. We have a golf cart, with my bag already on it, and a beautiful, uncrowded golf course just ten minutes away. The kitchen is perfect, with all the extras, and my home office is large enough to have clients visit and take advantage of the guest suite with its own spectacular porch view, mini-kitchen, and sitting area. There are several fireplaces inside to enjoy while watching the snow, as well as an outside fire pit for the deep, meaningful talks that happen best by open flames on a chilly night in the mountains.

Enough about my dream home! How is yours coming? Don't hold back. It's your home. Write down some of the details in your journal.

- Where is your dream home located? (Describe it in detail. Is it on a lake? In the mountains? On a beautiful beach?)
- How many rooms does it have?
- What surrounds your dream home?
- What special features does it have (private office, gourmet kitchen, fire-pit, swimming pool, and so on)?

Got it? Great. Now I want you to imagine you are at your dream home and you are sitting on the porch, looking at your favorite view. The weather is perfect, with a slight breeze. The sun is creating just the right amount of warmth. But it gets better. It is your birthday, and you are reflecting on everything you have to be grateful for. You smile as you count your blessings.

But it gets better. Not only is it your birthday, it's also the family reunion. Everyone you love and hold dear in life is celebrating with you. Not only your blood relatives, but also the friends and people you have "adopted" into your family. Your dream home is filled with life, and you are overwhelmed with gratitude for the sounds and smells.

But it gets better. It's not just any birthday, it's your eightieth birthday. Your mind is sharp, and physically you are doing well. As you smile to yourself, your countenance glows with contentment and with that "knowing" feeling that you have done everything you could to prepare those you love to navigate life after you are gone. You are 100 percent content and at peace with everyone you love and 100 percent sure of what eternity holds for you.

And then you hear it. Two of the great-grandkids are playing on the side of the house where you can see and hear them. The eleven-year-old boy from the East Coast asks his nine-year-old cousin from the West Coast the question: "Do you know the words our family stands for?"

"Yes!" she says, and she recites them.

Imagine if this happened to you. How would you feel?

I have good news for you. *You have a choice!* You can do today, and every day, the things that will build a legacy and ripple through eternity. It starts with hope. Without hope you won't even try.

Make sure you define success correctly, as this determines your direction and, ultimately, your happiness. Significance is where the joy in life is found—in helping others be, do, and have more than they thought possible.

Choose to Win: Transform Your Life One Simple Choice at a Time. Success and significance are stepping-stones on the way to legacy. When legacy is your *why*, the *how* and the *what* come to life. Let's get started!

Chapter 2

WHAT IS YOUR PLAN?

Replace a Bad Habit
with a Good One

I t all started with a question.

I remember the moment like it was yesterday. I was speaking in Melbourne, Australia, to 150 business owners and investors. Saturday, July 25, 2015, was a cool and crisp day, and the session was going beautifully. When I do full-day events, I give the group plenty of opportunities for questions. Halfway through the morning session, a thirtysomething man raised his hand and asked, "What is the fastest way to success?"

This may surprise you, but in my fifty years of experience in the personal and professional success field, nobody had ever asked me that question! (Clarification: I am fifty-four years old, so I am claiming fifty years of experience since Zig Ziglar is my father. Technically, I have worked in the industry for twenty-two years.) I had to think fast. About 150 sets of eyeballs were looking at me. Out of my mouth came these words: *"The fastest way to success is to replace bad habits with good habits."*

Next question please.

A short time later we took a break, and after we came back from the break the host of the event, Steve McKnight, led off the next session by recapping the morning session. I was leaning against the wall, waiting for Steve to bring me up, when he said, "Did you hear what Tom said just before the break? Write this down. Tom said, 'The fastest way to success is to replace bad habits with good habits.'"

When I answered the question in front of the group, it was a spontaneous answer brought forth by the pressure of the moment. When Steve quoted it, well, it sounded pretty smart. Even I wrote it down! As I progressed through the rest of the day, it kept popping up in my mind. I kept thinking I must have quoted someone else.

The first thing I did when I got to my room at the end of the day was google "Who said the fastest way to success is to replace bad habits with good habits?" There were multitudes of books and studies about habits and success. However, no one had said it as simply as I had.

Could this be true? Could I be onto something?

In all my years as the CEO of Ziglar, Inc., and knowing personally the greatest thinkers, researchers, authors, and speakers in the personal development world, I know that for something to be effective over a long period of time it must deliver at least three things. It must

- inspire hope,
- be based on truth, and
- be simple to implement.

Let's put my teaching to the test. If you simply replaced bad habits with good habits, and you did it often enough, would it change your life?

Isn't this the problem we all face? We know things could be better. In fact, we believe things *should* be better. We are *tired* of being sick and tired, of not having enough margin in our lives to breathe, of energy-zapping relationships, of not having enough money to do what we love to do when we want to do it. Yet every time we try to make a change or turn for help, we get overwhelmed with the complexity, the time commitment, the expense, and the radical requirements.

What if the answer were really simple and straightforward?

The very next day after the Melbourne program, I flew three and a half hours to Darwin for an event. Four days later I flew another three and a half hours to Sydney. Two days later I flew more than four hours to Port Moresby, Papua New Guinea, and then three days later I traveled twenty-three hours back home to Plano, Texas. On every leg of my travel, I tested and contemplated the sentence, and at every event I used it.

I applied the Wheel of Life my dad adopted to see if my statement held up. I applied my philosophy about habits to the Wheel of Life, and I made a discovery that is the core message of this book and is covered in section II, "The 7 Choices Plan." In that section, you will evaluate each of seven areas closely, identifying the habits you want to change. But before embarking on that life-changing plan, you need to understand the Wheel of Life.

THE WHEEL OF LIFE

The wheel is a simple yet profound way to get a snapshot of how well you are doing in life. Every dream or goal you have and every struggle you are dealing with will fall into one of these seven areas of life: mental, spiritual, physical, family, financial, personal, and career. To be truly successful, you need to be thriving in each of these seven areas.

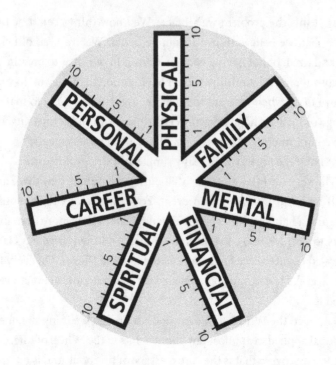

Since each spoke on the wheel represents one of these areas, in a successful life all the spokes would be the same length. If any of the spokes were shorter, then the wheel would no longer be round, and riding on that wheel would be very bumpy and uncomfortable.

Take a look at the diagram and quickly rate yourself in each area. Go ahead and mentally put a dot on the number on each spoke that reflects how well you believe you are doing. When you are finished, connect the dots from spoke to spoke.

How smooth is your ride? Do you have a flat tire? If you are struggling in any area, it will impact your whole life. To find out more, go to www.Ziglar.com/ChooseToWin and take the Wheel of Life assessment. It contains questions about each spoke of the wheel, and the results will give you greater insight into how you are doing.

The Discovery

What if you took each spoke on the Wheel of Life separately and simply replaced bad habits with good habits? What would happen?

- Would your mental life improve?
- Would your spiritual life improve?
- Would your physical life improve?
- Would your family life improve?
- Would your financial life improve?
- Would your personal life improve?
- Would your career life improve?

The answer? Yes, yes, yes, yes, yes, yes, yes! Seven times *yes*!

This discovery is a simple, proven way *you* can change and take control of *your* life.

It works because it is simple to implement.

....

The fastest way to success is to replace
bad habits with good habits.

....

I recommend focusing on replacing one bad habit with a good habit each week. Here's the weekly approach:

Each week identify a bad habit in a specific area of your life and replace it with a good habit in that area. There are seven areas in your life, so each week work on one area and then move on to the next area the following week. In seven weeks you will have made an improvement in every area of your life!

For example, if you are addressing the physical spoke of the Wheel of Life, perhaps you have the bad habit of drinking a soft drink each day, so you decide to replace that with the good habit of drinking a bottle of water every day for the entire week. When the second week comes, you continue this good habit and tackle another spoke of the wheel. At the end of seven weeks, you have replaced a bad habit in each area of your life with a good habit. At the end of a year, you will have replaced fifty-two bad habits with fifty-two good habits, and when you do this your life will be radically changed!

THE TERMITE PHILOSOPHY

....

"Hurricanes and earthquakes get all of the publicity,
but termites actually damage more homes—
and they take such little bitty bites!"

—ZIG ZIGLAR

....

I love the idea of little bitty bites. Having more success, creating a life of significance, and leaving a legacy all start with the right kind of little bitty bites. Have you ever been overwhelmed by the size of a project or goal? I know I have. "The Termite Philosophy" is all about breaking it down into little bitty bites. This simple idea, combined with replacing a bad habit with a good habit, is life-changing.

Think of it this way: When you have a bad habit, it's like digging a hole. A lot of bad habits create a really deep hole. Getting out of the hole means you have to stop digging *and* start building a ladder to get out.

Creating the life you want simply means replacing little bitty bad habits (stop digging) with little bitty good habits (building a ladder).

Rule 1: Stop digging!
Rule 2: Build a ladder!

Do you feel your hope rising? When you have a clearly defined *why*—to build success, create significance, and leave a legacy—and a simple game plan to get there, hope is created, and hope gives you the courage to try.

Choose to Win: Transform Your Life One Simple Choice at a Time will help you create a game plan so that you can create your dream life in the fastest way possible.

Remember: *the fastest way to success is to replace bad habits with good habits.*

What if . . .

- instead of drinking a sugar-filled soda, you were to drink a glass of water each day? Answer: you would lose seventeen pounds in a year (if everything else stayed the same).
- instead of not acknowledging your friends and loved ones, each day you wrote a note to someone telling them you love them? Answer: you'd be surprised how many people don't know that you care and will appreciate you even more.
- instead of not planning your day, you started each day with ten minutes of planning? Answer: you'd be amazed how many important things you get done.
- instead of having the smartphone at the dinner table, you made mealtime a smartphone-free zone? Answer: you would look forward to family mealtimes.
- instead of sitting for hours at your desk, you intentionally got up and moved for five minutes every hour? Answer: you'd come up with brilliant ideas because you were refreshed throughout the day.

IT'S A CHOICE

Your choices today become your reality tomorrow.

Choose to do the things today that create your success.
Choose to do the things today that forge your significance.
Choose to do the things today that establish your legacy.

When building your legacy becomes the direction you are headed, success and significance are part of the journey.

The *how* is simple: identify your bad habits and replace them with good habits.

TIME TO PONDER

Take a few minutes right now and ponder the next questions, then write the answers in your journal. Don't hurry. This is important!

- What legacy do you want to leave?
- What habits do you need to build this legacy?
- What habits do you have that are sabotaging your legacy?

Not sure? Stuck? That's okay. The rest of this book is a step-by-step guide on how to create the plan that will build the legacy you want to leave.

JUST START

A number of years ago, I attended the memorial service for Fred Smith, business executive and Christian layman. Fred was Dad's mentor and the wisest man I ever met. Fred lived an amazing life and influenced the who's who of influencers through his mentoring, writing, and speaking. At the memorial service, they played a video of Fred that he recorded not long before he passed away. In the video Fred explained that he learned the biggest lesson of his ninety-three years of living during the last year of his life.

For much of the last year of Fred's life he was a complete invalid, depending on his daughter Brenda for everything. Many days he barely had the strength to open his eyelids, much less turn over or sit up. Fred learned his biggest lesson during this time of complete physical dependence and exhaustion.

Fred said he would wake up in the morning with the realization that God had put something on his heart that he knew he had to do. He would then "negotiate" with God on why he couldn't do it: He was in pain. He had no energy. He felt horrible. He was exhausted. He was dying. And then Fred said he knew he would never win a negotiation with God, so he would call Brenda over and begin

> ....
>
> "When God lays something on your heart to do, your only responsibility is to just start. God doesn't give you the strength to overcome, He gives you the strength while you overcome."
>
> —FRED SMITH
>
> ....

dictating to her what God had laid on his heart. That was when it hit him: He simply needed to take action and obey. The results would be up to God.

What has God laid on your heart to do? What legacy does He want you to leave? You can often tell if it's from God by the size of it. God has God-sized plans for you. Your only responsibility is to *start*. So let's get started!

Chapter 3

GOALS

What Is Your *How*?

....

"If you aim at nothing, you will hit it every time."
—ZIG ZIGLAR

....

If you want to achieve success, significance, and legacy, then it's important you determine the goals you're aiming for. Goals carry out your vision for your life. They require a clearly identified target, a plan that will get you there, and the action steps to execute the plan. In other words, you first must commit to using a system, then you need to identify the steps for success in that system, and then you have to execute those steps. No system works unless you do.

There are many noteworthy goal systems available, but I believe the Ziglar Goals System is the most powerful and proven system in the world to turn dreams into goals and goals into reality. Let me give you some encouragement as to why you should choose this system.

Does making $100 a minute sound like a good use of your time? It does to me!

In January 2015, I was coaching Michael Watts, one of our Ziglar Legacy Certified Trainers. Michael explained to me that he wanted to grow his business revenue from $1.7 million, where he had been stuck for the previous four years, to $2 million in 2015. This would allow him to make a nice profit and pay some bonuses to his people. I agreed with him that this was a good goal and was very realistic, even though his industry, residential remodeling, had gone through tough times because of the economy and the housing mortgage crisis.

Michael put together a great strategy with three essential elements:

- Clarity: he knew exactly what he wanted to achieve, and why.
- A plan: the Ziglar Goals Setting System enabled him to create a plan he could execute daily and that was in his control.
- Accountability: he committed to reviewing his goals daily and to checking in with me on a regular basis. Michael specifically used the Ziglar Performance Planner to achieve this.

As the year progressed, Michael stayed on track working his plan. In October I called and asked for an update, and he said he was going to hit his goal of $2 million in early November. He was very excited! But not nearly as excited as when I spoke to him again in January 2016.

"Michael, how did you finish the year in 2015?"

"Tom, it was fantastic. We actually did $2.3 million for the year."

"Wow!" I said. "That is incredible. You had a very doable but aggressive goal for the year of increasing $300,000, which is an 18 percent increase. You doubled your goal! Almost a 36 percent increase!"

Then I asked him a question.

"Michael, I can understand how you went from $1.7 million to $2 million in sales. That's a big increase, but it was certainly achievable by staying focused. Now, can you tell me the one thing you did that allowed you to get the extra $300,000 and go from $2 million to $2.3 million in revenue?"

There was a long pause before Michael answered. Finally, he said, "Tom, the one thing I did that allowed me to earn the extra $300,000 was I reviewed my goals *every day.*"

"That's it?" I responded. "You give credit to the fact that you reviewed your goals every day without fail."

"Yes," he said.

My mind was racing. *That is way too simple,* I thought. Then I got excited.

"Michael, the $300,000 in extra revenue above your goal averages out to an extra $25,000 per month; since there are twelve months in the year, 12 x $25,000 = $300,000."

"Yes, Tom, that is correct."

"Michael, we know that people who review their goals daily will invest about six to ten minutes a day doing this. Would you say that this was true for you?"

"Yes, Tom, that sounds right. I reviewed my goals, updated my activities, and then listed my next important action steps. It really didn't take much time at all."

"So, what you are saying, Michael, is that you invested about eight minutes a day. An average month has thirty days in it, so that means you were investing 240 minutes a month in reviewing your goals. Do you realize what you just told me? For every minute you invested in reviewing your goals each day, you made $100 in revenue! That is incredible!"

Let me ask you again. Does $100 a minute sound like a good use of your time? Can I hear you say YES in all capital letters?

I am telling you this story about Michael Watts for a very simple reason: *you* can do what Michael did to achieve your own goals.

Michael did three very important things that all goal achievers do, which are part of the Ziglar Goals System:

1. He wrote out his goal in detail.
2. He worked on his goal every day.
3. He had an accountability partner.

What about you? Do you have a goal worth achieving? If the answer is yes (and I know it is), can you do those three things? Of course you can! Now, do me a favor: get your pen and your journal, and write down this phrase, including your goal: I can and I will [your goal]!

It just got personal, didn't it? If it sounds like I am talking to you, it is because I am. What I am about to share with you is life-changing—but only if you do it. Thinking about it will not change anything, but doing it will change everything.

The reality is, I don't think the idea of a goal-setting system is strong enough. Instead of calling it a "goal-setting system," I want you to think of it as a "how to get what I want" system. This is the beauty of systems. When you follow the system, you get results. When you don't, you don't. Once again, whether you do or don't is a choice, and the choice is *yours*!

MIND SHIFT: GOAL SETTER OR PROBLEM SOLVER?

What gets you more excited: setting and working on goals, or solving problems? I was having breakfast with one of my mentors, Bob Tiede, and he shared with me that only 20 percent of people are excited about setting and working on goals, while the other 80 percent are primarily motivated by solving problems. What about you? Would you rather identify and solve problems or work on goals? Since I learned this from Bob, I have spoken to numerous groups and asked them the same question. To my surprise, what Bob shared with me has proven true in my informal surveys. Eighty percent of people *do* prefer solving problems rather than working on goals.

....

"Identifying a problem is not negative, it's positive. It
only becomes negative if you continue to focus on the
problem instead of focusing on the solution."

—ZIG ZIGLAR

....

Did you get that? Identifying a problem is positive because you
can't solve it until you identify it. Good news. The Ziglar Goals Setting
System can easily be transformed into the Ziglar Problem Solving
System by simply substituting the words *problem solving* for *goals setting*. Either way, you win!

Think back to the story of Michael Watts making one hundred
dollars a minute working on his goals every day. If you prefer solving problems over setting goals, then do this mind shift regarding the
three things problem solvers (goal achievers) have in common:

1. Michael wrote his *problem* out in detail.
2. He worked on his *problem* every day.
3. He had an accountability partner.

Following is a quick overview of the seven steps that make up the
centerpiece of the Ziglar Goals System that Michael Watts followed.
Please notice how I have given you the option of being goal focused or
problem-solving focused.

Ziglar Seven Step Goals Setting
(Problem Solving) Procedure

Step 1: Identify your goal (problem to be solved).
Step 2: List the benefits of reaching this goal (solving this
problem).

Step 3: List major obstacles and mountains to climb to reach this goal (solve this problem).

Step 4: List skills and knowledge required to reach this goal (solve this problem).

Step 5: List individuals, groups, companies, and organizations to work with to reach this goal (solve this problem).

Step 6: Create a plan of action to reach this goal (solve this problem).

Step 7: Name a completion date.

As you can see, goals setting and problem solving are two sides of the same coin. It's your attitude and the action that follows that make the difference. If you love setting and achieving goals, go for it! If you love solving problems, go for it! Either way, the Ziglar Goals Setting/Problem Solving System will work for you.

MINDSHARE

Do you ever get stuck? You know you need to start working on the goal, taking action on your dream, but you just can't seem to start. Even if you know how to set a goal or solve a problem, nothing happens until you take action.

I was discussing this challenge with John Rouse, a coaching client who has become one of my closest friends. As we dug into this issue, we had a breakthrough that really helped him, and I believe it will help you too. Following are a series of questions I asked John that I want you to answer as well.

Tom: "I want you to think about the time you wake up every day. Your mind is either thinking about the past, the present, or the future. What percentage of your

mindshare is thinking about the past, what percentage
is thinking about the present, and what percentage is
thinking about the future?"

John: "I would say that 20 percent of my mindshare is
thinking about the past, 40 percent is thinking about the
present, and 40 percent is thinking about the future."

Tom: "Okay, good. When you are thinking about the past,
what percentage of your thinking about the past is positive
and what percentage of your thinking is negative? Positive
would mean you have a memory or an event that you are
grateful for, something you learned, something you believe
has made you a better person or is setting you up for
future success. Negative would mean a memory or event
that is holding you back that you believe is limiting your
future potential or is a reason you can't do something, or
is creating a current belief or emotion today that hurts
your ability to perform or enjoy life to its fullest."

John: "Twenty-five percent of my mindshare on the past is
positive, and 75 percent is negative."

Tom: "It's true there are things in our past that are hurtful and
painful. Mistakes we have made and wrongs that have been
done to us. In order to create the future we want, we need to
make friends with our past. We have to forgive ourselves and
others. We have to look at the negative events in a different
way. What did we learn? How can we use this experience to
make ourselves better? How can we use this to help someone
else? Most of all, we need to understand that how we see our
past is important because it has brought us to where we are,
but how we see our future is far more important. John, when
you start to have negative thoughts about the past, can you
start to reframe them and begin to use them as lessons you
can use to make a positive future?"

John: "I can do that. How do I start?"

Tom: "Start with gratitude. Acknowledge the good things you have learned from the past and recognize that not all the lessons were fun but, nonetheless, you are grateful for who you are today. Second, make sure you forgive yourself and anyone else who has caused you harm. This will help release you from the control the event or the person has over you. Forgiving them does not absolve them from their guilt, but it does enable you to move on. Finally, create a list of the things you have learned from the situation and recognize how this will make you better able to create the future you want. Recognizing we have the choice to see even the most negative things of our past in a positive way changes our thinking, and our thinking is the key to the future. John, you said that 40 percent of your mindshare was on thinking in the present. What percentage of this is positive, and what percentage of it is negative?"

John: "Seventy percent of my present thinking is positive, and 30 percent is negative."

Tom: "That is good, but I believe you can do even better. When your present thinking is negative, ask yourself why. Is it because of negative input or things that have changed your attitude? If so, take action and choose to input good, positive things into your mind through listening, reading, or interacting with positive inputs. If your negative thinking is due to a challenge or obstacle, go into goal-setting or problem-solving mode. Recognize that it is positive to identify a problem but negative to stay focused on the problem. Instead, get solution-focused and write down the various ways you can solve the problem, and then take action. Use the Seven Step Goal Procedure to do this if necessary. Does this make sense?"

John: "Yes, it does. I think I already knew this, but I don't always do it. I will make it a point to recognize a negative thought when I have it so I can address it right away rather than let it take over big chunks of my day."

Tom: "Perfect! That is an awesome habit to create. Change the bad habit of dwelling on the negative to the good habit of focusing and taking action on the solution. You also said that 40 percent of your mindshare was spent on thinking about the future. What percentage of this mindshare is positive and what percentage is negative?"

John: "Sixty percent is positive, and 40 percent is negative when it comes to thinking about the future."

Tom: "Tell me more about what your negative thinking is regarding the future."

John: "Something will go wrong and I will start to think about all the bad things that could happen. It could be a business challenge or a relationship problem. Before I know it I am consumed with all the things that could go wrong in the future. This can really derail me."

Tom: "This is my biggest battle as well. A lot of times a series of little things will send you on a negative time-traveling trip into the future, and before you know it you are homeless, friendless, and broke! I have awakened in the middle of the night more than once with worries about the future. Here is how I handle it, especially when my negative imagination has gone overboard:

"First, I get out my gratitude list and go over everything I have to be grateful for. I need to get my mind back on the right track, and the reality is, we all have so much to be grateful for. Keeping a gratitude list is one of my best habits. Once I have a good dose of gratitude, I dig into the worry or negative thought I have and turn it into a problem to be solved. I identify the problem and then write down the actions I can take to solve the problem. Now my mind is at ease because I have a plan and I can begin to take action. Of course there are problems none of us can solve, and these problems I turn over to God and focus on my faith. I do my part, and I trust God to do His.

"The key to mindshare is to make our thoughts about our past positive because we have learned and are benefiting from our past, and to move our negative thoughts about the future into problem-solving actions in the present. The present is the only place we can take action."

As we wrap up this chapter on your *how*, I want to remind you of a few things and then give you a great place to start.

Goals are powerful! Michael Watts made one hundred dollars a minute in revenue every time he reviewed his goals. You can have incredible results too. Most people would rather solve problems than set goals. That is okay! The Ziglar Seven Step Goal Setting (Problem Solving) Procedure works equally as well for achieving goals and solving problems. What matters is actually using the procedure.

Your mind is incredibly powerful, and how you invest your mindshare will determine how fast you solve problems and achieve your goals. Taking control of your positive and negative thinking in your mindshare is a choice that will transform your life.

THE FIRST THINGS FIRST GOAL

If you have never set a goal, I want to give you what I call "The First Things First" goal. It has four phases. You can start with the first phase, and once you get the habit of doing it daily, add in the next phases. Or you can start doing all four phases right away; it's up to you. The important thing is to start.

Phase 1

First thing each morning set aside a few minutes to review your goals and set your priorities for the day. Do this for several days or weeks until you are really comfortable with it.

Phase 2

Add a five-minute quiet time, such as the one I learned from the book *2 Chairs*, written by my good friend Bob Beaudine.[1] Each morning I set up two chairs, one for me and one for God. I then ask God three questions: *God, do You know what's going on?* (Yes, He is God); *God, are You big enough to handle it?* (Yes, He is God); *God, what is the plan?* Then I just listen. One minute of my thinking and asking and talking to God, and four minutes of listening. This has changed my life, and I bet it will change yours as well. If you do not believe in God, or you are unsure, use the time for reflection. Five minutes of reflection first thing in the morning will increase the clarity you need to have a productive day. Now, after your five minutes of reflection or *2 Chairs* time, work on your goals and priorities.

Phase 3

The mental model habit—this little habit is a real powerhouse! Each day, as you write down your goals and priorities (phase 1), also write down your meetings with other people and any presentations or calls you may have that are important to achieving your goals. Then invest one minute creating a mental model of how each of these is going to play out perfectly. Envision the best outcome and take into consideration the people you will be meeting with. For example, if your goal is to sell an idea to a few people in a meeting, envision what needs, wants, and concerns they may have. This way you are prepared in advance for the best outcome, and even if it takes an unexpected direction, you will have a better chance for a positive outcome.

Phase 4

Finally, add devotional, educational, and inspirational reading and listening to your First Things First routine. A few extra minutes will likely grow into thirty minutes or more. This is for your personal and spiritual development, and this time really creates fuel for your day.

Good news! First Things First is something anyone can do, and it takes only a few minutes each day in the beginning as you develop the habit of running your day instead of the day running you. Even if you start with just five minutes a day and add only a little bit of time each week, in just a few weeks you will see a profound difference in the outlook and results of your life. When you are practicing First Things First, you are choosing to win! It's a choice!

Are you ready to transform your life? Get ready! The Trinity of Transformation is described in the next chapter.

Chapter 4

DESIRE, HOPE, AND GRIT

The Trinity of Transformation

Are you ready to transform into the person God created you to be? As you prepare to embark on the 7 Choices Plan in section II, keep in mind the Trinity of Transformation. The Trinity of Transformation is a simple model you can use to help transform into the person who consistently enjoys balanced success, significance, and intentional legacy.

Picture in your mind a beautiful hot-air balloon. This is not just any balloon. This balloon can take you across the widest ocean and over the tallest mountain. The destination is up to you. How you live each day, the choices you make, the habits you create, and how you define success, significance, and legacy will determine which direction the balloon goes. If you are not intentional, the winds of life will take you to places you never wanted to go.

DESIRE

It starts with desire. Desire is the basket of the balloon. What do you desire for your life? First, let's be clear on what we mean by desire. I like what Noah Webster said about desire nearly two hundred years ago. He said, "Desire is a wish to possess some gratification or source of happiness which is supposed to be obtainable."[1]

As you imagine the balloon, I want you to picture in your mind the basket. This is where you will be riding. On the outside of the basket you clearly see the word *DESIRE* in big letters. Now is the time to clearly identify everything in life that you desire. Everything you want to be, do, and have. The more clarity you have, the more direct your journey will be. This will take some time, and this is why we covered goal setting in the previous chapter. Go ahead and fill up the basket with all your desires.

Now it's time to add more to the basket. Load into the basket all your gifts, talents, skills, and experience. Pay careful attention to your gifts and talents—you are the only person in the world with this unique combination, and they are key to your journey.

HOPE

Now something magical starts to happen. Your gifts and talents start to combine with your desires, and a flame is ignited. This flame starts to fill the balloon of hope!

What is it you really desire? When your desire is clearly defined, it focuses, harnesses, and influences the will and makes you proceed to action. Your willpower is largely determined by your desire. This is powerful! Desire creates action. Desire is what powers the daily habit of the right input. When desires get transformed into dreams and goals, action is the natural result.

When you fill the basket of your balloon with your clearly defined desires, it allows you to see a new vision of your future. Imagine when your desires come true. What will your life be like? How will things change? Once you start to imagine your desires into reality, it starts to fill the balloon of hope. While desire is the basket of the hot-air balloon, hope is the balloon itself.

As you begin to imagine what the future can become and reflect on your past victories and successes, the balloon of hope begins to fill. In fact, hope increases your desire, and desire increases your hope. Desire and hope go hand in hand and feed each other!

Hope is having confidence in a future event. For example, I have hope about the future because I believe in God's gracious promises never to forsake me.

The Trinity of Transformation starts with desire and grows with hope. Now the real work begins.

Transformation requires work. Desire gives you the clarity to see what you want, while hope gives you the belief you can achieve it. Grit is the action that makes it happen. Angela Duckworth, who wrote the book *Grit*, says grit is a combination of passion and perseverance.[2] I believe having grit means if you get knocked down 100 times, you have the strength of character to get up 101 times. Grit is that bulldog determination that says, "I am not stopping until I have completed what I set out to do." Grit ignores the world, the naysayers, the self-doubt, and the pain, and says, "Just one more time."

As you are standing in the basket, you look up as your beautiful balloon starts to fill. You notice that on the outside of the balloon is the word *HOPE* in huge letters. As the balloon continues to fill, hope starts to rise! The combination of your desires, your gifts and talents, and the higher altitude gives you a view and a perspective you've never had before. You are able to see the past and understand how all your experiences have prepared you for this day. You turn the other direction and see your future. You realize for the first time that, as my dad said, *"Your past is important, but not nearly as important as how you see your future."*

Your excitement grows as you realize the potential of your future. And then you notice the balloon is no longer rising. It's still above the ground, and the view is amazing, but the balloon needs more altitude if it's going to cross the oceans and go over the mountains you can see in the distance.

You take inventory of all your supplies: your gifts and talents, your skills and experience, and your desires. You realize that your dream life is on the other side of that mountain and your balloon is not going to make it. And that's when you notice the furnace of the balloon. On the furnace of the balloon is a knob that is labeled *Grit*.

GRIT

Grit. (noun) Courage and resolve; strength of character

Grit is doing the work necessary to achieve what you desire. Grit is the fuel in the furnace of your balloon. Desire lights the furnace. Hope keeps the fire of the furnace from going out. Grit is the fuel the furnace burns.

Grit is when you purposefully develop the skills, gifts, and talents God gave you that will allow you to achieve your goals and dreams.

Grit is the hard work of doing something poorly over and over again until you learn to master it.

Grit is the ten thousand hours of dedication to transforming into the person God created you to become.

You turn the knob of grit, and suddenly white-hot flames erupt from the furnace. The heat is intense, and the balloon shoots up, gaining altitude. This is when you fully understand that your balloon is fueled when grit is applied to your gifts and talents. Grit is awesome! The harder you work and the more focused you get, the more flames come out of the furnace. And then you notice something strange. When you apply grit to the gifts and talents God gave you, everything is great, but when you apply grit to areas where you don't have gifts and talents, the flames are barely visible. Quickly you learn to focus grit on your gifts and talents to maximize what God has given you. And then it happens—*bam!* Your balloon jerks to a sudden stop!

Your balloon is really struggling to gain altitude as the white-hot flame of grit is going full strength, but you are no longer rising! What could be holding you down? You gather up your courage and look over the side of your balloon and you see it. Your balloon is tied to the ground by several ropes! There is one more thing you have to do with your balloon for you to reach your full potential. You have to cut the ropes that are holding the balloon down. This takes more grit!

I call these ropes bad habits or the results of bad habits. These ropes include things like the bad habit of limiting beliefs, or bad health habits, or bad self-talk habits—really, any habit that prevents you from maximizing the gifts and talents God has given you. You grab the razor-sharp knife of wisdom, and with a lot of grit you start cutting those ropes.

As you cut the first rope you notice it is labeled *Limiting Belief.* As you cut the rope, you say out loud, "I can do this. What others have told me in the past is wrong. I am designed for accomplishment, engineered for success, and endowed with the seeds of greatness." When the rope is cut, the balloon jumps. You rise rapidly and then it happens again—*bam!*

You look over the side, and another rope is holding you down. This one is labeled *Bad Habit.* As you cut this one, you start to smile as you gain altitude. Why are you smiling? Simple—you see many more ropes, but you have a really sharp knife and a lot of grit. You are *choosing to win*! Your balloon is now gaining the altitude necessary to reach your goals and dreams!

Here's a quick recap of the practical and tactical view of transformation.

> **Desire:** Determine what you really want. This is the driving force that gets you started.
>
> **Hope:** Believe that achieving your desires will give your life meaning and purpose.
>
> **Grit:** Identify the skills, knowledge, attitudes, gifts, and talents you need to develop, and the bad habits and limiting beliefs you need to get rid of, and then work on them relentlessly until you become the person who can achieve your desires.

Let's make this personal. Take a few minutes right now and write down in your journal what *you* desire, what hope looks like to *you*, and what *you* need to work on with grit.

In the next seven chapters, we are going to go over the seven key areas in the Wheel of Life—mental, spiritual, physical, family, financial, personal, and career—and how you can maximize your success in each of these areas. As you digest each chapter, apply this balloon analogy to your life by asking these simple questions about each of the seven areas:

- What are my desires, dreams, and goals for my life in each area? (Desire)
- How will my life be better in each area when I achieve my desires? (Hope)
- How can I apply grit to my gifts, talents, skills, and experience in each area? (Grit)

- What ropes (old beliefs and bad habits) do I need to cut in each area? (Ropes)

CHOICES, CHOICES, CHOICES

At the end of the day, our future depends on the choices we make. Yes, *you can* transform your life one small choice at a time!

The Trinity of Transformation is powerful—but it depends on the choices you make.

Goal setting is powerful—but it depends on the choices you make.

Taking ownership of all seven areas of your life is powerful—but it depends on the choices you make.

Your future is up to you—and your future depends on the choices you make.

Here is the better-than-good news: you are about to dive into a proven life-changing plan that works because it identifies for you, and with you, the small choices you can make in all seven areas of your life that will add up to produce the life God created you to have.

Transforming yourself, and your life, starts with the right input. The challenge we all face is having the internal motivation to make seeking out the right input a lifelong habit. The right input doesn't happen by chance; it happens by choice. We may be blessed with people in our lives who do all they can to give us the right input, but there always comes a day when we have to take responsibility for this ourselves.

Today is your day! Today is the day you officially take responsibility for choosing the right input, and this simple choice, followed by action, will change your life forever!

Write the following commitment in your journal, inserting the date and your name:

Today, _____(date), I, _____ (your name), will choose the right input to put into my mind. I understand completely that my future results are based on the habits I create, and the most powerful habit of all is choosing the right input that powers all my other habits.

Let's get started! After all, the life you want is a choice!

THE 7 CHOICES PLAN

*Transform Your Life, One
Small Choice at a Time*

The heart of *Choose to Win* is about the small choices we make daily. The reality is we make our choices, but we don't get to determine the consequences of our choices. Once the choice is made, the consequences are set in motion.

The good news is that most of the time we can predict what the consequences of our choices are likely to be, and we can change our direction by making new choices! This book is about showing how you can take control of your life, one small choice at a time, so that success, significance, and legacy are predictable outcomes.

"You can't determine your future, but you can determine your habits, and your habits will determine your future. Your habits are *choices*."

I strongly believe that if you make enough good small choices in every area of your life, the result will be the life you have always dreamed of. The next seven chapters are in a specific order on purpose, because the right choices done in the right order create a solid foundation, build momentum, and allow you to overcome the adversities of life.

Don't be overwhelmed. A good habit is simply a good small choice done over and over again.

Go ahead, choose to win; after all, the choice is yours!

Chapter 5

MENTAL

Choose Your Input

CHOICE 1: The mental input, what you choose to think about, determines everything about how you live.

....

"You are what you are and where you are because of what has gone into your mind. You can change what you are and where you are by changing what goes into your mind."

—ZIG ZIGLAR

....

This quote from my dad is one of my favorites. In simple, precise language it tells the story of you and me. We are the sum of all the things that have gone into our minds and what we believe about those things. The quote offers incredible hope as well. If you don't like who you are or where you are right now, that's okay. You can change what goes into your mind from this moment on, and that will change who you are and where you are.

....

"Your input determines your outlook. Your outlook determines your output, and your output determines your future."

—ZIG ZIGLAR

....

INPUT DETERMINES EVERYTHING

Why is it that almost everyone allows others to determine their input? How about you? Do you choose your input, or do you abdicate that responsibility?

A number of years ago, I knew I had to lose some weight. I will talk more about this in detail in chapter 7, but here is the essence of how I was able to lose more than fifty pounds. I started reading and listening to every health-related item I could find. Every day my input was focused on learning what was good for my health. What I should eat. How I should exercise. Without even realizing it, my thinking and habits changed. I started wanting the healthy choice, and I started craving the next healthy thing I could do. Because my input changed, my outlook, my output, and my future changed.

This experience led to this belief: *"What you feed your mind determines your appetite."*

I shared this quote at an event in Atlanta and a lady sitting in the back of the room stood up and said, "That's just like NASCAR!" The last thing I was thinking of was NASCAR when I said that.

"Please tell me how that quote is like NASCAR," I said.

"That's easy," she said. "In NASCAR, the drivers go around the track at over 180 miles per hour. That is so fast that their eyes have to be focused on where they want the car to go. At that speed, if they look at the wall, their hands will make an involuntary micro-adjustment to follow their eyes and they will hit the wall."

Wow! She was right. Isn't it true that we go through life telling ourselves, "Don't eat the cheesecake, don't sit around all day, don't worry about that," and what we end up doing is eating the cheesecake, sitting on the couch all afternoon, and complaining to our friends about a problem we have no control over? We need to be solution focused, not problem centered. This can only happen when we choose to feed our minds the right things.

Still a little skeptical? Imagine you have a seventeen-year-old daughter, or a favorite niece, and she has just started dating. She is the apple of your eye—innocent in every way, and her whole life is ahead of her. You want the best for her, and you have done your best to guide her in making good decisions.

Now imagine a new eighteen-year-old boyfriend is taking your princess out on a date. You are in the kitchen and you hear the boyfriend pull up in his "classic" Transmaro (Transmaro = half Trans Am/half Camaro). The boy is forty-five minutes early, which is odd, and then you notice he is just staying in his car, listening to really loud music. After thirty minutes you decide to do a little recon of the situation.

You walk around the back of his car in his blind spot to see what he is doing. As you peer through the window, you notice he is transfixed on his smartphone—watching porn! Question: Does he get to take your princess out on a date that night? Absolutely not! After all: *what you feed your mind determines your appetite.*

It just got real, didn't it? Now you know why Super Bowl ads go for millions of dollars.

HOW PURE IS TOO PURE?

If someone told you they were going to give you three pounds of gold, what purity level of the gold would you want? Fifty percent? Ninety percent? No, you would want as close to 100 percent as possible. The purer the gold, the more value to you. Your brain weighs about three pounds. Would you sell your brain for three pounds of pure gold? Of course not! Your brain is priceless. Question: Why would you allow anything to negatively impact the purity of your brain? The input that you choose to allow into your mind impacts your choices, and your choices determine your outcome.

Are you ready for a transformation? The reality is, every single one of us has had things happen to us that are not good, that tear us down, that if we accept as "this is just the way it is" will limit our potential and negatively impact our future. The good news is *you* can make a *choice* right now to change your input and change your beliefs about what has happened to you in the past.

FACTS VERSUS PROBLEMS

I learned this bit of wisdom from Dad's mentor, Fred Smith. There is a real difference between facts and problems. Facts, we have to accept; problems, we have a choice. A fact is something we can't change, no matter how much we want to. With problems we have a choice. We can choose to use the problem as an excuse, as a reason why we can't. Or we can get solution focused instead of problem focused and figure out ways to accomplish our goals despite the problem.

Several years ago I had the opportunity to participate in a Ragnar Relay race from Miami to Key West, Florida. The route we ran was almost two hundred miles! I was invited to participate with the Operation GiveBack team. Operation GiveBack was founded by my good friend Jose Garcia-Aponte, CSM US Army, retired. Their mission is to raise awareness and resources for our wounded warriors, their families, and the children of our fallen heroes. On our team were the most amazing men and women I have ever encountered. These men and women were either currently serving in the military or were veterans who had been injured serving our country.

As an able-bodied civilian, I felt out of place. I had never put my mind and body through a thirty-four-hour, 196-mile relay race, living out of a van, getting almost no sleep, and I was surrounded by real-life heroes. My body ached from head to toe, and my calves had golf ball–size knots in them. Yet I didn't dare complain.

I would look over at Chris Gordon, Will Castillo, and Lito Santos, who had each lost part or all of one of their legs in combat. How could I complain about knots in my leg when they didn't have a leg? Not only that, but I didn't hear them complain one time. Instead, I saw them serving one another and even asking me how I was doing. I marveled that these men, who had already given so much, were putting themselves through more pain to raise money for the kids of our fallen heroes who had paid the ultimate sacrifice. In the midst of their own pain and trials they were still serving others.

Fact: they had each lost a leg.

Problem: walking was going to be difficult, slow, and painful.

Solution: come prepared with the right attitude, start early, bring extra meds and bandages, and focus on the needs of others.

Lesson learned: when the *why* is big enough, the sacrifice is worth it.

What *facts* do you need to accept so you can "move on" (for example, divorce, lost job, or disability)?

What *problems* have these facts created for you (for example, physical limitations, financial, mind-set, or beliefs)?

You have a choice. You can choose to allow the problems to be an excuse for why you can't do something, or you can become solution focused and choose to do it anyway.

- You can choose the right input, which will change your attitude, beliefs, and mind-set.
- You can choose to start earlier, work longer, and bring the meds.
- You can choose to have a *why* bigger than yourself.
- You can choose to transform yourself into the person God created you to become.

Living to win is a choice! What choices are you going to make right now that will transform you? Write at least three in your journal.

Now that you have made the choice of the right input, you have lit the fire in the furnace of your life. Now we need to make sure the fire doesn't go out! To fuel your fire, you will need the Trinity of Transformation—desire, hope, and grit—that we covered in chapter 4.

Remember the hot-air balloon example? It has three major components: the large balloon where the hot air is trapped, allowing the balloon to rise and take you to your destination; the basket of the balloon that holds you; and the furnace that transforms the fuel into fire, which heats the air in the balloon. Your balloon is unique—the only one in the world capable of taking you to the life you want and the dreams you have. Now that you have made the choice to choose the right input (the fuel) and the fire is lit, you need to start choosing the right input!

Choosing the right input isn't complicated. All you have to do is ask yourself this simple question: Is what I am

- reading,
- viewing on the internet (social media, etc.),

- listening to,
- watching on TV,
- discussing with a friend, coworker, or family member, and
- saying to myself in self-talk,

bringing me closer to achieving my desires, creating more hope that I can achieve my desires, and adding to what I need to develop with grit?

Yikes! That is a tough question, isn't it? I said it was a simple question, not an easy question.

Now that you have identified what your Trinity of Transformation looks like, it's time to build some mental muscles and exercise the right input. The workout formula is something we have already covered. Here it is again: *the fastest way to success is to replace bad habits with good habits.*

Get your pen out—it's time to take action!

THREE QUESTIONS TO TRANSFORMATION

In each of the chapters about the seven areas in the Wheel of Life, I want you to write your answers to these questions in your journal. Clarity helps you make the right choices and take the right actions!

1. What are my desires, dreams, and goals for my mental life? (Desire)
2. How will my life be better in the mental area when I achieve my mind-set desires? (Hope)
3. How can I apply grit to my gifts, talents, skills, and experience in the mental area of my life? (Grit)

Now it's time to develop the strategy and take action!

Step 1: Identify the Bad Mental Habits You Have

What input is going into your mind, either purposefully or accidentally, that is negative and keeping you from achieving your desires, dreams, and goals (internet, social media, negative relationships, books, radio, TV, self-talk, and so on)?

Write them down in your journal and be specific.

Step 2: Identify the Good Mental Habits You Need

What input can you purposefully put into your mind that will allow you to achieve your desires, dreams, and goals faster (education, online courses, positive relationships like mentors or coaches, books, podcasts, self-talk, and so on)?

Write them down in your journal and be specific.

Step 3: Choose to Replace a Bad Mental Habit with a Good Mental Habit

Pick a bad habit you want to replace with a good habit. Start small and build up. The key is starting and sticking with it! Each week you build on the same change from the previous week or replace another bad habit with a good habit.

Example: In the mental area of your life you identify the bad habit of watching too much TV—more than two hours a day. Week one your goal could be to replace fifteen minutes of TV with listening to a podcast that will educate and inspire you to help you achieve your desires, dreams, and goals. This may not seem like much, but when you add to this every week, before you know it your life will be completely changed!

Bad mental habit: watching too much TV.

Good mental habit: intentionally put good, clean, pure, powerful, inspirational, and educational information into your mind.

Here are four examples of how you can make small choices that will transform your life.

Example 1: Reduce TV time from two hours to an hour and forty-five minutes a day and listen to an inspirational, educational podcast fifteen minutes a day.

Example 2: Reduce TV time from one hour forty-five minutes to one hour thirty minutes a day and read an inspirational, educational book fifteen minutes a day.

Example 3: Change my self-talk by stopping negative self-talk and replacing it with reading one of the Ziglar Self-Talk Cards each morning with my coffee, which takes three minutes a day. (The cards are printed in the back of this book, or you can download them at www.ziglar.com/ChooseToWin.)

Example 4: Stop my negative self-talk whenever it happens and read my Ziglar Self-Talk cards out loud each morning with my coffee and each night right before I go to bed, which together takes six minutes a day.

Every week you keep or build on the previous week's change. You are building good habits because you are making good choices!

Write down what you are going to intentionally do. Remember, the goal is to replace a small bad habit with a small good habit, and to do this over and over again until you transform into a completely new person.

In your journal list the bad mental habits you are going to get rid of and then list the good mental habits you are going to implement. Write down your daily action plan to implement at least one good mental habit.

This may not seem like much, as it usually takes only a few minutes a day to implement a small good mental choice, but when you add to this every week, before you know it your life will be completely changed!

Can you feel it? Hope is rising because you are starting to get clarity on where you want to go, and you have identified the choices you need to make to get there! Your balloon is starting to take flight!

....

Chapter 6

SPIRITUAL

Choose Your Principles and Values

> **CHOICE 2:** The spiritual principles and values you choose to live by either limit or unleash your potential.

....

"The most important persuasion tool you have
in your entire arsenal is integrity."

—ZIG ZIGLAR

....

When we choose the right input, we have taken the most important step we can take in determining the right outcome. But what is the right input?

The right input is spiritual input. Spiritual input includes our faith, or to a nonreligious person, our system of belief. Spiritual input includes the principles and values we choose to believe, and the character qualities we choose to live by and develop in our own lives. I have met people who claim great spiritual faith, yet seem to have no principles and values. I have also met people who do not claim any spiritual faith, yet live their lives with high moral standards, principles, and values.

As a follower of Christ, I can tell you that my success in life, and the balanced success I have, is not because I am a Christian. It is because I make choices to follow what Christ said, even though I have to admit I am not always perfect. The standard is high indeed.

As we dig into the spiritual area of life, we are going to focus on what we call the Qualities of Success. The Qualities of Success are the character qualities that all of us have within us. To transform our lives, we need to make intentional choices to develop each of these qualities. I believe character qualities are spiritual.

Spiritual is not physical, yet spiritual soundness largely determines physical results. My friend and mentor Rabbi Daniel Lapin uses the following illustration to explain the difference between physical and spiritual: "A violin is physical. You can touch it, and it can only be in one place at one time. If beautiful music is played on the violin, the tune is now in the heads of everyone who heard the music. When they leave the concert, the tune is now in hundreds of heads in hundreds of locations all at the same time. The music is spiritual."[1]

Character, integrity, principles, and values are spiritual qualities. Dad was famous for saying, "You can't do a good deal with a bad guy." On paper the math may work and the physical components may make sense; but if the deal is with a "bad guy," then it is only a matter of time before spiritual corruption destroys the deal, and when the deal craters, it is simply the natural result of poor choices regarding character, integrity, and dozens of other spiritual character qualities.

The good news is, you *can* do a good deal with a *good* guy!

MAKING IT RIGHT

....

"I will make it right."

—HOWARD PARTRIDGE

....

In 2011, our company was going through a transition and looking for the next opportunity. Dad's speaking career had come to an end, and we needed to plan for the future. The family owners of the business—my sisters, Cindy Ziglar Oates and Julie Ziglar Norman; my niece, Katherine Witmeyer Lemons; and I—went to Chicago to invest a full thirteen-hour day with a business consultant whose expertise was looking at all the current assets of a business and then recommending the greatest opportunity for the future.

At the end of the day, he said, "Ziglar has a huge opportunity to work with small-business owners and to help them become more successful. They share the same philosophies and values that Ziglar has, and what you have already developed and what you already teach is perfect. However, you need to develop new practical and tactical content that a small-business owner can use to run their business in *all* areas of the business—sales, marketing, operations, administration, and leadership."

Our family left that meeting energized—and overwhelmed! We already had a great deal of the needed content, but we also knew it would take several years to develop the new courses and learn how to market to small-business owners. On the drive back to our hotel, we discussed the possibilities, and within a few minutes Howard Partridge's name came up.

We had been working with Howard for about two years at this time, and we knew that he already had these business systems developed and had hundreds of success stories from business owners who had used those systems over the previous fifteen years. Because we had been working with him, we knew firsthand that what he was doing worked. I gave Howard a call before we returned home to discuss the possibilities. I have to tell you Howard got very excited.

During the next few months, we started digging into what this partnership would look like. I also made several trips to Howard's live events and started reflecting on his previous events I had attended. I started to see a pattern. A pattern I liked. I would ask his clients what they liked about Howard and his program, and they all said the same three things:

- "I love Howard." Now, that is an interesting thing to say first about a business relationship, isn't it? After all, love is a spiritual quality. Howard's clients really do love him. Love is a result of actions that come from the right motives and are supported by character and integrity.
- "Since we started working with Howard, our business has made more money than ever before." This was the answer I thought would be number one. Howard was helping them get results, and this is the type of partner we were looking for.
- "Since we started with Howard, we have more time to spend with our families." Wow, this one blew me away. This is exactly what we teach in everything we do, and it was one of the top three benefits listed by Howard's clients. No wonder they loved him! He was giving them their families back!

As we dug deeper into the relationship, we realized that we were teaching almost exactly the same things, and in many other areas, we each had tons of content where the other didn't have much. Everything was lining up perfectly. And then I asked him the following question. "Howard, if we do this partnership together and we send you all our clients, I am sure there are going to be occasions when our client joins the new program, and then, for whatever reason, they want their money back. Maybe it's just not a fit, or maybe there is no reason and they just want their money back. How will you handle that?"

Howard looked me in the eye and said, "Tom, I will make it right." We officially began our partnership that day.

For the past seven years, that is exactly what Howard has done. Hundreds and hundreds of clients. Thousands of interactions. Howard and I have traveled the world doing hundreds of events together. Whatever the situation, Howard has made it right.

So, what does it mean to "make it right"? Clearly, "making it right" falls into the spiritual category. It is far more than physical. The physical you can touch, see, hear, smell, and taste. Making it right is a feeling. You can do the job correctly, but I still may not trust you, and you may not have integrity or character. If you have character and integrity and do the job wrong, you can come back, make it right, and I will trust you—maybe even more because you lived up to your word!

In order for "I will make it right" to really work, there has to be a benchmark higher than ourselves that we agree is the standard. If "make it right" is left up to my definition, based on how I am feeling at that moment, then trust will never occur because there is no agreement on what integrity really means. This is why the focus of this chapter is on character and integrity and the choices we make to live by principles and values. Making it right in every area of your life requires a commitment to the principles, values, and character qualities that, when lived by, automatically produce good results.

QUALITIES OF SUCCESS

Long-term balanced success requires spiritual soundness. Spiritual soundness comes when you recognize and develop the Qualities of Success that are within you. For decades, at Ziglar we have taught and trained individuals, small businesses, Fortune 500 companies, educational institutions, the military, and local, state, and federal governments this concept, both in the United States and all over the world. In our "politically correct" world, you may wonder how we are able to teach these spiritual concepts. Let me explain a common objection we face and how we handle it.

On more than one occasion, we have prepared a very large training proposal for a Fortune 500 company that is hypersensitive to the "PC police." After we present our proposal and show them how we can help them get the results they are looking for (higher productivity, reduced turnover, increased sales, more bottom line profit, better culture, and so forth), someone on the decision-making committee will often raise this objection: "Wasn't Zig Ziglar a Southern Baptist preacher, and don't you teach principles and values from the Bible? We can't have any religious teaching in our company."

At Ziglar Corp, we love this question. Here is our answer:

> Zig Ziglar was a sales professional, business owner, speaker, and writer, but he was never an ordained minister. Mr. Ziglar did teach Sunday school. It is true that the principles and values we teach are found in the Bible; however, in our corporate training we do not reference the Bible in our materials. Instead, we reference the principles and values that we call the Qualities of Success. We believe that people already have these Qualities of Success within them, and that they only need to be brought out and developed so that they can maximize their potential and improve their performance. Here is what we are willing to do. We have compiled a list of sixty-eight Qualities of Success that we teach. Why don't you go through the list and circle the ones you don't want us to teach, and we will take them out.

And then we hand them this list:

THE QUALITIES OF SUCCESS			
character	integrity	honesty	gratitude
intelligent	teachable	passion	convictions
goals	dependable	encourager	organized
vision	pride	responsible	diligent
commitment	faith	thrifty	manners
punctual	resourceful	self-starter	extra-miler
wisdom	courage	confident	sober
optimistic	enthusiastic	loyal	smart
motivated	respectful	hard worker	decisive
caring	humble	authoritative	focused
self-control	affectionate	disciplined	supportive
fair	sincere	communicator	positive mental attitude
persistent	consistent	attentive	team player
personable	creative	energetic	open-minded
knowledgeable	competent	good finder	humor
self-image	educated	common sense	good listener
teacher	obedience	service attitude	trustworthy

Would you hire someone to be on your team if they were a ten out of ten in every one of these qualities? Of course you would!

Now look at the list again and get your pen out. Write in your journal the ten Qualities of Success that you believe are the most important to your long-term success. Now go back through the above list again and write down in your journal the ten Qualities of Success you believe you need to develop the most in your life right now, ones that you feel need improvement. For me, the quality I am always working on is discipline. I confess that often I know what to do, yet often I don't do it.

I know this lack of discipline is largely a choice. Discipline may not be "natural" for me, but I have created many good habits based on choices that automate discipline in my life. The Perfect Start in chapter 12 is one of these choices that allows me to have discipline, even when it's not natural for me. Now look at the Qualities of Success that you wrote in your journal. This is a great place for you to start. What can you put into your mind that will help you develop these qualities?

THE QUALITIES OF SUCCESS ARE ALL CONNECTED AND COMBINE TO IMPROVE YOU SPIRITUALLY

Whenever you begin to develop one of your Qualities of Success, it impacts in a positive way your other Qualities of Success. For example, working on discipline makes you more trustworthy, focused, confident, diligent, and responsible, just to name a few.

Several years ago I had a conversation with Seth Godin. I consider Seth a friend and a mentor, and I have read his blog[2] every day for many years now. I asked Seth what his current focus was, and he told me it was the scalability of trust. He explained that his priority in every business interaction was to scale trust, and if trust grew, then his business and, more important, his influence and relationships, would grow.

In 1984, Dad wrote the book *Secrets of Closing the Sale*, which has sold well over a million copies. In the book Dad talks about the five reasons people do not buy a product or service: no need, no want, no hurry, no money, no trust. The biggest of these reasons is no trust! Now look at Seth's wisdom. His priority is to scale trust, and by doing so he eliminates the biggest reason people will not do business with him. When you have trust with a prospect or client, all that is left to do is to find solutions to the problems they are facing.

The scalability of trust concept helped me link two other pieces of information: a TEDx Talk about the biggest predictor of happiness and my dad's Sunday school class called the Encouragers Class.

In the TEDx Talk, Dr. Robert Waldinger, the director of the Harvard Study of Adult Development, discusses one of the most comprehensive longitudinal studies in history, often referred to as the seventy-five-year Harvard study.[3]

The researchers gathered data from a group of more than seven hundred men over a period of seventy-five years, from their teen years until today. Interviewing the men every two years about all areas of life over the course of seventy-five years produced an incredible amount of information. The researchers asked the men if they were happy and satisfied with their lives. They compared the responses of the men in their eighties with the responses the same men had given when they were in their fifties, and what they discovered was profound. The secret to being happy and satisfied with your life is to focus on relationships. Not on career, or money, or influence, or fame, but on relationships!

One thing that every good relationship has is trust between, and for, each party. Relationships are built on trust, and trust is a spiritual quality. You may not call yourself a religious person, but principles, values, and character qualities like trust are necessary to build great relationships. People with good relationships can still bicker and argue with each other, but at the end of the day their bond is cemented by their trust for each other. So how do we build trust?

....

Trust is the by-product of integrity.

....

In order to create a relationship built on trust, we have to live lives of integrity. If we don't have integrity, we can't create trust. I love Noah Webster's definition of *integrity*. He said it is "the entire, unimpaired state of any thing, particularly of the mind." Integrity "comprehends the whole moral character," but it has a special reference to dealings between people, companies, and nations.[4]

Trust is the by-product of integrity. Good relationships are built on trust, and trust comes from integrity. Where does integrity come from? I believe integrity comes from truth. Where does truth come from? As a Christian, I believe truth comes from the Author of truth—God.

As I began to reflect on the TEDx Talk by Dr. Waldinger and the concept of the scalability of trust by Seth, it seemed so familiar. As I dug deeper, it took me back in time almost thirty years ago when I would attend the Encouragers Sunday school class Dad taught. Every Sunday Dad asked the class two questions before he started his lesson: "How many of you read the Bible every day this week?" (Only about 30 percent of the hands went up!) "How many of you practiced good biblical self-talk every day this week?" Biblical self-talk is simply when you repeat a Bible verse to yourself, but you make it personal by putting it in first-person, present tense. Psalm 23 works well: "The LORD is my shepherd; I shall not want" (v. 1).

Here is the *aha* for you. If you want to create a happy, satisfying, balanced, and successful life, focus on relationships. Relationships are built on trust, and trust is the by-product of integrity. Integrity is built on truth. What Dad was teaching was simply the reverse. Put the most powerful truth (God's) into your mind by using the most powerful method available (your voice), and this will build your integrity, which will allow you to create relationships built on trust, which will allow you to have a happy and satisfied life.

Everything is connected! As we develop our spiritual Qualities of Success, everything in our lives improves. When we choose the right input, especially input that builds our Qualities of Success, we choose a better future. This is much more than knowledge; this is wisdom. Knowledge is the accumulation of information; wisdom is the application of this information in the form of life-transforming choices.

As a young boy I asked Dad a question: "If you follow God's Word but don't believe in God, what happens?" Dad's answer was simple: "Making wise choices based on principles and values will give you the benefits of those choices, even if you don't believe in God."

Imagine that in your business you have a key customer who represents more than 50 percent of your revenue. Now imagine that you have to assign an account manager to work closely with this key customer, and how well the relationship goes will determine the success or failure of your business. The catch is you only have two candidates to pick from.

The first candidate has thirty years of industry knowledge and knows every technical aspect the client could ever need. However, that person is lacking in their Qualities of Success, and their integrity and trust-building capacity is questionable. The second candidate has invested a lifetime developing their Qualities of Success; however, they are brand-new to your industry and have much to learn when it comes to industry knowledge and technical expertise. Which person would you choose? The one with knowledge, or the one with character and integrity? It's an easy choice, isn't it?

WHAT CHOICES ARE YOU MAKING?

When I was sixteen years old, I applied for my first "real" job: selling shoes at the Athlete's Foot in the mall. As I was filling out the job application, I went to Dad to get his help. "Dad, what do I put in the experience section? I have none." He smiled at me and said, "Son, you have sixteen years of experience working on discipline, a good attitude, hustle, character, and integrity, just to name a few. Write that down."

I got that job!

Are you choosing to work on the most important things first? Our physical abilities diminish with age. Skills and knowledge required to thrive in our world today are changing rapidly. The reason we stay in good shape and constantly develop our skills and knowledge is to maximize the impact of our Qualities of Success. Our priority is to develop who we are first. Who we are, being the right kind of people with good principles and values, allows us to make right choices and good decisions.

A LITTLE CHANGE CAN MAKE A HUGE DIFFERENCE

Years ago I was working a product table at a seminar we were holding in Eugene, Oregon. We had about eight hundred in attendance that day, and during one of the breaks, a man came over to look at our offerings. He had a big smile on his face, and I could tell he wanted to talk.

"How can I help you?" I asked.

"These programs are fantastic," he said as he looked at everything we had on the table. "What Mr. Ziglar said changed my life."

"That's great!" I replied. "What did he say that changed your life?"

"He said so many things that rang true, but one of them really hit home. I was struggling in my relationships at home, at work, and socially. Mr. Ziglar said that we should be completely honest with ourselves when we evaluate everything we do. My problem was I believed I needed to tell people what they wanted to hear, so I developed the habit of telling little white lies on just about everything. When my boss asked if the report would be finished on Wednesday, I told him yes, even though I knew it would be Friday. When my wife asked if I would be home for dinner at six, I told her yes, even though I knew it would be seven. In my mind, I didn't want to disappoint them when I was talking to them, so I told them a little white lie. Mr. Ziglar said we should always just tell the truth.

"I decided to give complete honesty a try and it changed everything! The next time my boss asked if the report was going to be done on Wednesday, I told him the truth and said it would be Friday. When I turned it in on Friday as promised, he actually thanked me and let me know he didn't really care when I turned it in, but he needed to know when it would be done so he could plan his other work. When my wife called to confirm I would be home for dinner at six, I told her I was running behind and it would be seven. When I got home at seven, she thanked me and told me she didn't really care what time we ate, she just wanted to eat together when the food was still warm. This simple concept changed all my relationships and gave me the proof I needed to take the rest of the advice Mr. Ziglar gave."

Integrity, character, honesty, and all the spiritual Qualities of Success are the foundation for a successful life. Are you ready to build a rock-solid foundation for your life?

The fastest way to success is to replace bad habits with good habits. Get your pen out—it's time to take action!

THREE QUESTIONS TO TRANSFORMATION

For each of the chapters on the seven areas of the Wheel of Life, I want you to write down your answers to the questions in your journal. Clarity helps you make the right choices and take the right actions.

1. What are my desires, dreams, and goals for my spiritual life? (Desire)
2. How will my life be better in the spiritual area when I develop character, integrity, faith, and all the qualities that allow me to become the person God created me to become? (Hope)
3. How can I apply grit to my gifts, talents, skills, and experience in the spiritual area of my life? (Grit)

Now it's time to develop the strategy and take action.

Step 1: Identify the Bad Spiritual Habits You Have

What bad spiritual habits of either omission or commission do you have that are keeping you from developing your spiritual Qualities of Success like faith, character, integrity, love, compassion, and kindness, and that are negative and keeping you from achieving your desires, dreams, and goals?

Write them down in your journal and be specific.

Step 2: Identify the Good Spiritual Habits You Need

What input can you purposefully put into your mind, and what actions can you take that will strengthen the spiritual qualities you want to develop that will allow you to achieve your desires, dreams, and goals faster (for example: education, online courses, positive relationships like mentors or coaches, books, podcasts, self-talk, and actions you can take)?

Write them down in your journal and be specific.

Step 3: Choose to Replace a Bad Spiritual Habit with a Good Spiritual Habit

Pick a bad habit you want to replace with a good habit. Start small and build up. The key is starting and sticking with it. Each week you build on the same change from the previous week and/or replace another bad habit with a good habit.

Example: In the spiritual area of your life you identify the bad habit of being too self-centered and not focusing on the needs of others. You determine that life has become so hectic that your time and attention are far too focused on getting the next thing done rather than building the relationship right in front of you. You decide you want to develop the spiritual qualities of kindness, gratitude, and being a good listener so the relationships in your life improve.

Bad spiritual habit: self-centered and unintentional about growing relationships.

Good spiritual habit: develop the spiritual qualities of gratitude, kindness, and listening so my relationships improve.

Here are four examples of how you can make small choices that will transform your life.

Example 1: Each day write down the name of one person you are grateful for. Write down why you are grateful for him or her in your journal and thank God for that person. Name one person a day for two weeks.

Example 2: Go back through your list of who you are grateful for and send them a text or a card, or give them a phone call, telling them you are grateful they are in your life and telling them why. Do this for one person a day for two weeks.

Example 3: Ask each person on your list a "tell me more" question and listen to his or her answer—and even jot down the key parts of the person's answer in your journal. Example: "John, I know you really like to travel to Europe. Can you tell me more about why you like to do that?" Ask one person a day for two weeks.

Example 4: Make "tell me more" and words of kindness and gratitude part of your daily routine. Each day do not go to bed until you have intentionally done at least one of these three things once during the day. Do this for sixty-six days—the length of time it takes for this life-transforming small choice to become a habit.

Choose to win! Time to take action. Write down in your journal what you are going to intentionally do:

- Bad spiritual habits you are going to get rid of.

- Good spiritual habits you are going to implement.
- Daily action plan to implement at least one good spiritual habit.

This may not seem like much, as it usually takes only a few minutes a day to implement a small good spiritual choice, but when you add to this every week, before you know it your life will be completely changed!

Can you feel it? Hope is rising because you are starting to get clarity on where you want to go, and you have identified the choices you need to make to get there. Your balloon is starting to take flight and gain some altitude!

Chapter 7

PHYSICAL

Choose to Be Persistent and Consistent

> **CHOICE 3:** Your physical body is your engine. How persistent and consistent you are in fueling your body will impact your performance in every area of your life.

....

Change starts with you, but it doesn't start until you do.

....

How is your physical health? Regardless of our genetics and other things beyond our control, we can make choices that will improve our overall wellness. When we make these choices, it impacts every area of our lives. Almost nothing we can do gets faster results and bigger returns than focusing on transforming our physical lives one small choice at a time. The key to this is PC—persistent consistency.

I mentioned this in chapter 1, but it bears repeating. Several years ago I asked Dad a question: "Dad, I have heard you say a thousand times that the number one reason you are successful is because of your character and integrity. What would you say is the number two reason for your success?"

Dad's answer: "Persistent consistency. Consistency is when you have a worthwhile goal or objective and you work on it every day or as often as necessary. Persistent is when you take that work 'up a notch' each time you do it."

Persistent consistency, or PC, as we like to say, is the Ziglar definition of a good work ethic. You can apply PC to every area of your life and get results. This is especially true in the physical area of your life.

BAAM!

One of the best stories to demonstrate PC is the famous "Block and a Mailbox" (BAAM) story that my dad shared about his own health and weight-loss journey. When he was writing the book *See You at the Top* in the early 1970s, he realized he had a problem. In the book he was telling people, "You can do what you want to do, you can go where you want to go, and you can be who you want to be." The only problem was he weighed about thirty-six pounds too many, and his health was not what it should have been. Because of this, he made the choice to lose the weight and keep it off. The first thing he did was go to the Cooper Aerobics Center, founded by Dr. Kenneth Cooper, and get checked out by the experts and then get on a sensible exercise and eating plan.

As a seven-year-old, I vividly remember Dad going out for his jogs. Many times growing up I would go with him, riding my bike as he jogged. Persistent consistency was the secret to his success, and it started with a BAAM!

Here is the simple plan that made BAAM a legend. Dad determined and set a goal to exercise five days a week. Then Dad made the choice to do *a little bit extra* every time he jogged. The first day he jogged, Dad made it one block before he had to stop. Yes, he was in terrible shape! The second day he jogged he made it a block and a mailbox (BAAM). The third day he jogged a block and two mailboxes. And the next day a block and three mailboxes. Dad kept on PCing until he made it all the way around the entire block, and then two blocks, and then half a mile, and then one mile, two miles, all the way past five miles.

Notice the sequence of Dad's story. His first choice was to get the right *mental* input. Not only did he go to the doctors, but he started reading and learning everything he could on physical health. Then he reinforced his commitment around the *spiritual* qualities of consistency, discipline, and being persistent, which all help to build character and integrity. Then he did the *action* of exercise with PC. Because he made the right mental and spiritual choices first, the physical followthrough was much more likely to be sustained. Dad kept in good physical shape for the next forty years as he continued to exercise and eat right with PC.

There is another part of Dad's BAAM experience that is not well known. After he had spent several months eating right, jogging, and getting in shape, Dad ended up in the ER with severe abdominal pain. The doctors couldn't determine exactly what was wrong with him, so they admitted him to the hospital for testing and observation.

After five days and Dad getting worse, they performed exploratory abdominal surgery and discovered he had a ruptured gallbladder. They did everything they could to get the poison out of his system and then performed another surgery—to remove the gallbladder—a few days later after he was much stronger. The doctors told us that Dad nearly died, and he most likely would have died had he not been in good physical condition.

Because Dad was listening to God's nudges about what he should do, he was better prepared when the crisis came. Not only that, but the doctors didn't allow Dad to travel for six weeks, which meant his schedule opened up and he used that time to get laser-focused and write the bulk of a book you may have heard of: *See You at the Top*.

PUTTING PC AND BAAM INTO ACTION

Are you listening to God's nudges? Is your mind churning about how you can use PC and BAAM to totally transform your life? PC and BAAM are two of the concepts we teach to those who attend our Ziglar Legacy Certification (ZLC) course. One of the questions we ask the class is, "Do you have your own BAAM story of how PC helped you achieve a goal?" One of our ZLCers, Heather Prichard, raised her hand and shared her story with us.

As a seven-months-pregnant young woman, Heather had an AVM rupture in her spine. She nearly lost her life and was paralyzed from the waist down after she gave birth to her baby girl. The doctors told her she would never walk again. Heather had other ideas! She set a goal to walk before her newborn daughter did, and then she started the extremely difficult and painful regime of physical therapy. Every day was about PC—doing just a little bit more. After she was finally released from the hospital, her rehab continued at home.

Each day, with assistance and the help of a walker, she would use every ounce of her strength to walk just a little bit farther. These walks would take her outside, and her goal was just to make it to the next mailbox on her street. The story of Heather's courage and goal had gone before her, and as she began her daily rehab, the neighbors on her street would come out, each standing by their own mailbox. They would speak encouraging words to her, and as she made it to their mailbox, they would greet her with cookies, drinks, and other treats. Heather made her goal, and today she walks unaided on her own everywhere she goes! She has a beautiful family, an amazing career in real estate, and is a sought-after speaker, trainer, and coach.

If Heather can, you can—as long as you do what she did. Heather had a huge *why*: her newborn baby girl. She had the right mind-set, which was the result of choosing the right input that developed her attitude and her spiritual Qualities of Success. And then she took action with PC. Yes, you can do more than you think you can—just like Heather!

Persistent consistency is such a powerful concept for our physical health, and the good news is that PC, when applied, can change every area of our lives. Years ago, I was headed to Las Vegas with Dad for a big convention where he was speaking, and I was along to help support him and sell product.

As we took our seats on the plane, Dad started into his four-step routine. First, he got out his manila folder with the work he wanted to do on the plane and put it next to him on the seat. Second, he spoke to the flight attendant, got her name, and then let her know his seat belt was fastened, he was going to take a nap, and he was fine and didn't need anything. Third, in about sixty seconds, he fell asleep.

People boarded the plane, the plane taxied and took off, and Dad was sound asleep the whole time. Once we hit a high enough altitude, the wheels of the plane folded underneath and the sound of the hydraulics woke Dad from his nap. The last step of his routine was simple. He picked up his folder, put the tray table down, and started working. Yes, with more than thirty years' experience of traveling on airplanes (at that time), Dad knew how to maximize every situation. Not one second lost in achieving efficient productivity!

Watching this scenario unfold led me to my next question: "Dad, what are you working on?"

"I am working on my speech for tomorrow."

"Dad, you must have given this same speech well over a thousand times now. Why are you working on it again?" (I knew the answer, but I wanted to hear it one more time when I was really listening.)

"Two reasons, son. Number one, it will be the very first time some people in that room will have ever heard me. I have to be the best I have ever been. If I am, maybe, just maybe, one person in that room will take an idea I give them, and that idea will change their life. Number two is I am working on several things to customize this speech. I had a phone call two weeks ago with the CEO, the VP of sales, and the VP of marketing for the company where I'll be speaking. This is their big sales and marketing meeting to kick off the year, and they shared some key words and strategies that I want to include in my speech. Plus, I was reading some information in the news that applies to their industry, and I want to include some of that information in the talk. If I do this little bit extra, then maybe someone in the room will realize I customized this talk just for them, and it will inspire them to take action on an idea I give them, and maybe that will change their life."

Do you see the PC in action? Dad studied and prepared at least three hours for every speech he gave, even if he had given that same speech a thousand times before. This is consistency. Then he "took it up a notch" and added a "little bit extra" to the presentation. This is persistently adding a "mailbox" to his speech.

You overcome life's greatest challenges and you build a career, a life, and a future by combining your Qualities of Success with persistent consistency.

THREE KEYS TO PHYSICAL HEALTH: SLEEP, DIET, AND EXERCISE

When you use PC to maximize your physical health, you turn your body into a high-performing, dream-achieving machine. Is this how you view your body? You should! Your body is more than just a transportation device for your brain. It is the power plant that fuels your capacity to develop into the person God created you to be.

Your body is incredibly important, and you need to understand the difference between what it wants and what it needs. The bottom line is your body acts much like a spoiled two-year-old. It wants maximum gratification with minimum pain and expense. "Give me what I want right now! And just bring it to me!" What your body needs, though, is enough good sleep, the right kind of nutrition, and the right amount of exercise.

You have a choice to make. Are you going to take orders from a two-year-old, or are you going to choose to win by building a high-performing, dream-achieving body and enjoy the best physical health possible? After all, every bite you take, every minute you exercise (or don't), and how much sleep you get is a choice. I know that every now and then things happen beyond your control when it comes to how much time you have to sleep and exercise, but we have far more control over these things than we realize. Now is the day you take ownership of your physical self and use PC to transform your life. Let's dig into sleep, diet, and exercise.

Sleep

When I was doing research on the best habits we can develop to create good physical health, I was surprised to learn that getting enough good sleep is more important than your diet or how much exercise and movement you get.

According to research published in the *Annals of Internal Medicine*: sleep impacts your eating patterns; many people crave a carb-filled sugary snack to boost their energy when they haven't had adequate sleep. Lack of sleep also changes the fat cells in the body, making it difficult to lose weight and causing fat to be stored in the wrong places. Further, a study published in *Nature Communications* found that just one night of sleep deprivation negatively affected complex decision making, but lack of sleep also increases your desire for food and decreases your desire to exercise.

Key learning point: if you had to choose between eating right, exercising, or getting enough sleep, the best choice would be to get enough sleep!

I don't know about you, but setting a goal to sleep at least seven hours a night sounds really good. The benefits are amazing: more energy, more clarity, better decision making, easier weight loss, losing ugly unhealthy fat, more willpower, better chance of exercising, and better health. Add all this up and it's clear that when you get enough sleep, you feel better, you get more done, and you are more likely to follow through with your eating and exercise plans, which allows you to maximize your full potential.

Choosing to get enough sleep has a positive ripple effect in every area of your life. Now let's look at small habits you can create that will increase the quantity and quality of your sleep. The Sleep Foundation recommends certain habits to increase the quantity and quality of sleep, such as maintaining a regular sleep schedule every day of the week, doing a relaxing activity before bedtime, avoiding naps during the day, and exercising regularly. It's also important that your sleeping area is free from distractions and bright light, is set at a comfortable sleeping temperature (between 60 and 67 degrees), and is equipped with a comfortable, supportive mattress and pillows. (For more tips, go to https://sleepfoundation.org/sleep-tools-tips/healthy-sleep-tips.)

As we wrap up this section on sleep, I want you to do a quick sleep assessment. Please match each of the following statements with the answer—*never, sometimes, often,* or *always*—that best describes you.

I get at least seven hours of quality sleep every night.

I wake up fully rested and ready to tackle the day.

My family and friends would agree that I get enough sleep.

I believe the amount of sleep I am getting is maximizing my potential.

Do you see some room for improvement in your sleeping? If yes, that's good news, because when you choose to get the right amount of good sleep, you are choosing to live to win.

Diet: The Pure and Simple Approach

My goal in this section is not to advocate for the diet of the month but to give you a new way to look at what you eat. I have struggled with my weight my entire life, since the time I was a little boy buying clothes from the "husky" section. My body is a master at converting processed carbohydrates into fat. I have been as many as seventy pounds overweight and, until recently, have carried an extra twenty to thirty pounds around with me. Let me share my personal story.

In June 2007, I got sick and tired of being sick and tired. It seemed that life was just throwing its oozy, crummy, icky stuff at me. Of course, that is the nature of life, but why was so much of it sticking to me?

Even though I have been blessed with growing up in the "garden of Eden" when it comes to positive environments, and even though I am the CEO of "Motivational Mecca," I had been doing some things that made it easy for life's problems to knock me off my feet.

First, the surface area of my body was *way* too big. Being five nine and weighing 255 pounds created a lot of extra area for that slime to land on! Plus, the stuff I was putting into my body just wasn't good. Have you ever had a shirt that collected lint or hair as if there was a reward for it? Well, the food I was eating was pretty much collecting tiredness and grumpiness as if I was going to win a big prize for it!

Like many people, or should I say most people, I had pretty much tried all the diets out there. I knew another diet wasn't for me. I had been working out for years, two or three times a week. That's impressive, isn't it? Of course, my goal when working out was to make sure I didn't sweat and that I burned just enough calories to justify the lunch buffet that day.

Based on these obvious facts, I knew I had to change what I ate. Realizing my seemingly unlimited capacity to ignore the obvious, I made the foundational decision to change the way I looked at food. I called it the Purity Diet. And I made it very *simple*.

It works like this:

Pure food = GOOD
Impure food = BAD

What is pure food? Pure food is simply food the way God made it. No chemicals, no preservatives, no refining or processing, as raw and natural as possible. Things like fruits, vegetables, nuts, grains, and all kinds of meats.

The big difference is the no-processing and chemicals part. I now eat as little bread, pasta, flour, and other processed foods as possible. I am also picky about the oils I cook with. No artificial sweeteners either.

Did it work? I lost seventy pounds without ever being hungry.

Here are the questions I ask myself about food, and I ask them in this order:

1. Is it pure? See definition above. If yes, proceed to number 2.
2. How many calories does it have? Nuts are pure, and they have lots of good calories. Vegetables are pure, and they have low calories. The key is balance and variety. Make low-calorie, high-nutritional choices when possible.
3. Is it organic or grown locally? Number 3 is the bonus question. I don't go crazy on this one or limit myself if it's not organic or grown locally. But if you have the choice, this is better.

For the last ten-plus years, this has been my basic game plan. Eat pure food the way God made it. I haven't always been 100 percent consistent with it, and whenever I drift away and put on some extra weight, I go back to this approach and it works every time.

Here are several diet and nutrition habits I highly encourage you to follow.

- *Start with a doctor who understands science and wellness.* Being well doesn't start with a pill. It starts with the choices you make about what you put into your mouth. Pure food, the right amount and right kind of calories, and the right supplements all come together to give you the best chance for optimum physical health. Understanding this, and understanding that everyone is unique, means that your doctor should help you create a plan based on *you.*

- *"What you feed your mind determines your appetite."* This quote of mine is literally true. When you fill your mind every day with health information and education about what you should do and eat, your appetite changes. When you understand that a highly processed carbohydrate snack laced with sugar and chemicals gets converted to a slippery, stringy fluid called mucus that is stored in your cells, you lose your appetite for that kind of snack. When you focus on what you should eat, you suddenly make good, pure choices most of the time.

- *Know yourself.* I have learned that my body loves intermittent fasting. My goal is to have my last food by 7:00 p.m. and not eat again until lunch the next day. My clarity and energy go way up, and I am not hungry. My body benefits from the rest and restoration. (Note: I still drink black coffee and water in the morning.) Recommendation: ask your doctor about this for you—and if your doctor doesn't know much about this, then perhaps locate a doctor who does.

- *Plan ahead.* Map out each day so you can make sure you get the right kinds of pure foods. I travel a lot, so I plan on taking the right kind of snacks with me, mainly nuts. This keeps my energy up and my hunger down, allowing me to make good choices even when the circumstances don't give me many options.
- Make it a habit to ask yourself this question: *Is what I am about to eat going to move me closer to or farther from my health goal?* That's a tough question! But well worth asking.

As I started learning more about the negative health impact that preservatives have on us, I started thinking about bread. People ask me what I eat and what I don't eat. The biggest change for me has been bread. I don't eat much bread anymore unless it is unprocessed, sprouted bread like Ezekiel Bread.

"Where do you find that bread?" is usually the question. "You find it in the freezer section," I say, "because it is unprocessed and doesn't have preservatives in it like most bread, so it will get moldy very fast."

Most people think moldy bread is bad. I remember when I was a kid, our bread would get moldy after just a few days. Now it can be literally weeks before the bread turns green. Fact is, the bread has so many chemicals in it, the mold is just too smart to eat it! Imagine that—mold having more sense than we do when picking out bread. Here's a good rule of thumb when choosing food: if it's not good enough for mold, it's not good enough for you!

In my quest for eating pure, I also decided to stop using all artificial sweeteners. Since I love iced tea, especially with spicy food, this was a big deal for me. A typical lunch or dinner would consist of five or six glasses of tea, each one getting about three of those little packets of the artificial stuff.

When I made this change, it wasn't because of all the scientific studies on the possible harm that artificial sweeteners could cause; it was simply because eating pure food, the way God made it, and then adding a chemical to it just didn't make sense to me. I discovered pretty quickly that when you eliminate artificial sweeteners, you also eliminate a ton of their chemical buddies. Just check out the label on a diet soft drink and you will know exactly what I mean.

At first this was a pretty tough change for me. Tea just didn't taste the same. After the first week my tea was just barely tolerable. After the second week tea tasted okay. After the third week I was looking forward to tea again, and by the end of the fourth week I realized I would never go back. In fact, every now and then I accidentally take a sip of artificially sweetened tea and I can't stand it! It's like my mind is screaming, "Intruder alert! Intruder alert!" when the artificial stuff hits my tongue.

(As an additional note, I decided not to use sugar as a sweetener either. The fact that it is refined, has zero nutritional value, and is high in calories made this an easy choice for me.)

Two Unintended Amazing Benefits

When I started, I went cold turkey off the artificial sweeteners, and in less than forty-five days it became part of my normal life. I didn't really think much of it until the first Thanksgiving after I stopped using them when we had a potluck lunch at the office. My sister (thank you, Cindy) brought in baked sweet potatoes. I had never liked sweet potatoes, so it had been several years since I had even tried one. For some reason I decided to have one. I ate it plain—no butter, no sugar, nothing but a pure baked sweet potato. I thought I was in heaven when that first bite went into my mouth. It was so sweet I couldn't believe it. It felt like I was eating a dessert!

That is when I realized that because I had cut out the artificial sweeteners, my taste buds had come to life. All of a sudden it made perfect sense why fruit was tasting so much better and was so much more satisfying. All through my dieting life I had heard the word *satisfying* used to describe what a good meal should be. Until that point, I don't think I ever really understood what "satisfied" felt like.

Here is the second unintended benefit. This is not a scientific fact, but it's a theory I really believe in. After that Thanksgiving meal, I realized that my sweet tooth had gone away and that when I had sweet food like fruit or that baked sweet potato, I felt extremely satisfied. I believe that artificial sweeteners trick your brain into thinking you are getting the real deal, and when the brain realizes it was tricked, it sends signals for more sweets and it usually sounds like this: "Give me something sweet, *now!*" Yes, that two-year-old can really scream!

For years I thought picking an artificial sweetener was saving me calories and satisfying my cravings. Instead, it was just filling my body with junk, ruining my taste buds, and increasing my cravings for more junk. This reminds me of a great biblical illustration. I have heard it said that every person has a need for God that only God can fill. We don't like that, because admitting it means we can't fix our own problems, so we go through life filling that need with the artificial sweeteners of life—our work, more money, more stuff, alcohol and drugs, selfish relationships centered around lust, just to name a few. We crave more and more, we indulge more and more, and we are never satisfied.

Artificial is artificial—and *never* satisfying.

Take a quick diet assessment:

I eat a well-balanced "pure" diet every day: *never, sometimes, often, always*

After I eat I have more energy and zest for life: *never, sometimes, often, always*

My nutritionist would be proud of my diet: *never, sometimes, often, always*

I believe the food I am eating each day is maximizing my potential: *never, sometimes, often, always*

Do you have any room for improvement in the diet category? When you choose the right food, you choose to live to win!

EXERCISE (DO I HAVE TO?)

Some people love to exercise. I don't—until I am actually exercising! What about you?

....

"Logic will not change an emotion, but action will. Do it, and you will feel like doing it."

—ZIG ZIGLAR

....

For all my adult life, regardless of the type of exercise I was doing—weightlifting, walking, interval training, stretch bands, push-ups, planks—it has always been hard for me to get started but easy to keep going. The following is my philosophy on exercise and some principles that will change your life if you follow them.

Take the long view. My goal is to be chasing my great-grandchildren all over the beach and through the mountains when I am in my nineties. That means I have almost forty years to get ready, and my body needs to be as injury-free and in as good shape as possible when I get there. What is your long-term goal when it comes to your physical health?

Because of this long-term view on physical health, I know I need to create the habits today that will help me be the person in my nineties who can chase my great-grandkids. Here are some questions to ask yourself about exercise:

- Will doing this exercise help me avoid injury or increase the odds of an injury?

- Can I continue this exercise into my hundreds?
- Do I have the time and the resources to do this exercise daily at home and when I travel?
- Does this exercise build muscle strength and/or cardio health?
- How often do I need to do this exercise to achieve good, healthy fitness?
- *Bonus question:* Can I replace a bad habit with this exercise?

I like what Tom Rath says in his book *Eat Move Sleep: How Small Choices Lead to Big Changes.* Tom was a guest on our Ziglar Show podcast[1] and he talked about how as a society we just don't move enough. Many of us sit at a desk or in front of a screen for five, six, or even nine or ten hours a day. He points out that even thirty minutes of exercise five days a week has a hard time overcoming this reality. But there is something we can all do—we can choose to move!

I love this approach because it answers all the questions above with a capital YES! Here is how it works and what I am doing (even as I work on this book). I set the timer on my phone for every hour, and then I move with purpose for five minutes. My daily goal is to do this six times per day. At home or at the office, I make going up and down the stairs part of this movement.

Here are just a few of the benefits:

- It gets my heart rate up and my blood flowing, and my breathing is deeper.
- My posture is improved.
- I have more energy when I'm done.
- I have better clarity.
- I often do this instead of a snack, and I forget about the hunger craving.
- It's a good time to digest, think, and plan my next activity.
- I add to it the good habit of drinking some water.

- Many times I ask friends or coworkers to join, resulting in better relationships.
- I don't sweat! So I can go back to work right away.

Over time:

- Fitness goes up.
- Weight and inches go down.
- Blood pressure improves.

Another reason I like this approach is there are so many things you can do beyond just a purposeful walk.

I urge you to find an exercise program that works for you. The one I use was created by my good friend Scott Eriksson and is called NERDbody. You can find out more about it at www.NERDbody .com. I love the name NERDbody—because of the success I've had with the program, I can proclaim that I'm proud to be a nerd! When you become a part of NERDbody, you automatically get four text messages a day, and each message has a one-minute video demonstrating a simple exercise you can do with resistance bands, and each exercise takes less than two minutes! With NERDbody, in just a few minutes you are safely building muscle tone without sweating. NERDbody can be done by anyone, the resistance bands are inexpensive and travel easily, and there is almost no chance of injury.

Is your mind racing now? There are so many things you can do five minutes at a time that will really impact your life—and allow you to maintain fitness into your hundreds!

If traditional workouts of forty-five minutes, five days a week work better for you, that is great. My point is this: whatever you do, do it with PC and do it for the long term!

Take a quick exercise assessment:

I exercise or move daily as part of my routine: *never, sometimes, often, always*

My posture and fitness level give me plenty of energy: *never, sometimes, often, always*

My doctor approves of my weekly exercise and movement: *never, sometimes, often, always*

I believe the movement I am getting each day is maximizing my potential: *never, sometimes, often, always*

Do you have any room for improvement in the exercise or movement category? When you make daily movement and exercise a habit, you choose to win.

The fastest way to success is to replace bad habits with good habits. Get your pen out—it's time to take action!

THREE QUESTIONS TO TRANSFORMATION

I want you to write down the answers to these questions in your journal. Clarity helps you make the right choices and take the right actions!

1. What are my desires, dreams, and goals for my physical life? (Desire)
2. How will my life be better and different in the physical area when I fuel and support my body with the proper amount of sleep, food, nutrition, movement, and exercise that will allow me to become the person God created me to be? (Hope)
3. How can I apply grit to my gifts, talents, skills, and experience in the physical area of my life? (Grit)

Now it's time to develop the strategy and take action!

Step 1: Identify Your Bad Physical Habits

What bad physical habits do you currently have with your sleeping, eating, nutrition, movement, and exercise that are keeping you from living life at your full potential and achieving your desires, dreams, and goals?

Write them down in your journal and be specific.

Step 2: Identify the Good Physical Habits You Need

How can you improve the amount and quality of sleep you receive, the nutrition and food you eat, and the movement and exercise you do each day? What actions can you perform daily, and what input can you purposefully put into your mind, that will strengthen your physical health and allow you to achieve your desires, dreams, and goals faster (such as, amount of sleep, health education, online courses, positive relationships like nutritionists, doctors, trainers, mentors or coaches, books, podcasts, self-talk, and actions you can take)?

Write them down in your journal and be specific.

Step 3: Choose to Replace a Bad Physical Habit with a Good Physical Habit

Pick a bad habit you want to replace with a good habit. Start small and build up. The key is starting and sticking with it. Each week you build on the same change from the previous week and/or replace another bad habit with a good habit.

Example: In the physical area of your life, you identify the bad habit of not doing anything intentional to create good, balanced, overall health. As a result, your energy is low, you are tired most of the time, and you need to lose some weight. You realize that even little setbacks drain you and you absolutely must make a change before serious damage is done to your body. You decide you want to develop the good physical habits of getting enough sleep, eating healthy food, and getting enough movement and exercise.

Bad physical habit: no intentionality in sleeping, eating, or exercising.

Good physical habit: develop and implement a good sleeping, eating, and exercising lifestyle so your good health will allow you to achieve your desires, dreams, and goals.

Here are four examples of how you can make small choices that will transform your life.

Example 1: Determine what time you need to go to bed each night to get a solid seven hours of sleep. One hour before bedtime, start the sleep routine of unplugging from electronics and putting your mind at rest. Commit to making this your daily routine for sixty-six days.

Example 2: Identify the top five negative food choices you are making and replace them with five positive food choices; then exchange one bad choice for a good choice once a week for five weeks. Instead of a sugary soda each day, replace it with a bottle of water; or instead of a package of chips each day, replace it with some nuts.

Example 3: Replace the bad habit of sitting all day with the good habit of putting some movement into your day. Set your phone alarm for every ninety minutes, and when it goes off take a five-minute walk, do some stretches, and practice some deep breathing. Another option is www.NERDbody.com, which is an automatic service that sends you a text four times a day with a simple two-minute workout anyone can do.

Example 4: Change your mental diet and read or listen to at least one thing a day that educates you on health and wellness. Make "tell me more" and words of kindness and gratitude part of your daily routine.

Choose to win! Time to take action. List in your journal what you are going to intentionally do.

- Bad physical habits you are going to get rid of.
- Good physical habits you are going to implement.
- Daily action plan to implement at least one good physical habit.

This may not seem like much, as it usually only takes a few minutes a day to implement a small, good physical choice, but when you add to this every week, before you know it your life is completely changed!

Can you feel it? Hope is rising because you are starting to get clarity on where you want to go, and you have identified the choices you need to make to get there. Your balloon is starting to take flight and gain some altitude, because now you are fueling your health which, in turn, fuels every area of your life!

Chapter 8

....

FAMILY

Choose to Be a Positive Influence by Being a Good Example

> **CHOICE 4:** The *family* choices you make will set the example and influence you want to be for your loved ones.

Making good small choices on a daily basis sets in motion a legacy of transformation. It's important that we teach our kids to do what is right. It's even more important that we do what is right because "what is caught is more powerful than what is taught."

....

When we lead by example with what we do and with what we say, our influence is multiplied.

....

I learned habits from my dad that he never taught me. Growing up, it always amazed me how Dad got up so early to do his work. Reading, writing, and researching were things Dad did almost every day, and he started doing them long before the sun was up.

I remember one day early in my work career when I called Dad about 7:20 in the morning. I had a question for him (plus, I wanted to let him know I was at the office early). I remember making a point of telling him that I was calling him from the office. We had a nice visit, and then I asked him how his morning was going.

"Son," he said, "this morning has been fantastic. I have already done almost three hours of work. I have added a new wrinkle to my speech, and I have gotten a lot done on the new book." I remember hanging up and wondering how he did all that.

I don't believe he ever told me I should get up really early to start my day. Now I do exactly the same thing. In fact, the vast majority of this book was written before 9:00 a.m. Yes, Dad never "taught" me the habit of getting up early, but his example and his influence made sure I "caught" this wonderful habit.

A number of years ago, I was cleaning out the trunk of my car and I came across a folder and a notepad. I opened it and discovered several pages of notes and ideas I had written from a seminar I had attended. Immediately I was transported in my mind back to that day almost a year earlier. It was a great day, and the speaker was incredibly knowledgeable—a true expert. As I read through the notes I started thinking, *Wow, these are good ideas! I should do them.*

This is the moment when I asked myself the big question: *Why hadn't I already done them?* How about you? Have you ever asked yourself the same question? I then started to compare this to the impact my dad had on me. Over the years, tens of thousands of people have reached out to us with the same basic story: "I heard Zig Ziglar speak. I started doing what he said. My life is changed forever."

The life change only happened *after* they did what he recommended—change starts with the thinking and comes after the doing. What made them "do what he said"? I believe the two key words are *influence* and *example*.

In a general sense, *influence* denotes power whose operation is invisible and known only by its effects, or a power whose cause and operation are unseen. An example is a pattern or person worthy of imitation.

With family, it starts with the example we set. This is why we covered the mental, spiritual, and physical chapters first. When these three are on track, then we are becoming a successful person who is automatically setting the right example. Dad certainly set the right example! But how did he get so many people to take action on what he was teaching?

Influence is simply when you get someone to take action. I believe the two keys to positive influence are *hope* and *identity*.

Let me set the scene. For more than four decades, millions of people heard Dad speak, and most of the time there were more than ten thousand people in the room. For those hearing him for the first time, I can imagine their self-talk: "Wow, this is a lot of people. I heard Zig Ziglar was good, I sure hope he is. Hey, he is pretty good, and funny too! Wow, I bet he has the life—smart, funny, great speaker. I bet he is rich. I could never be Zig Ziglar."

And then Dad would ask those two questions I mentioned in chapter 1: "Is there anything you can do in your personal life, family life, or business life in the next week that will make things worse? Can I see your hands?" The crowd would always laugh as the hands went up.

"Okay then. Is there anything you can do in your personal life, family life, or business life in the next week that will make things better? Can I see your hands?" All the hands would go up.

And then Dad would say: "Whether you realized it or not, you determined in your own mind that you have the power to make things better or worse, and the choice is yours." This is where hope is born.

The first step in positive influence is showing people they have the *choice* to make things better or worse. This choice creates hope. This choice gives them power, and hope gives them the courage to step out and try. One of the most powerful things we can do for ourselves, and for our families, is to always focus on the choices we can make right now that will improve our situation. Go ahead and claim this power, and hope will be born in your life!

The second step in positive influence is the concept of identity. Dad told his story almost every time he spoke: He was born in LA (lower Alabama), then moved to Yazoo City, Mississippi. His father died when he was five, and he was raised by a single mom with a fifth-grade education in the heart of the Great Depression. He went to work selling peanuts on the street corner when he was six, never did well in school, went into the navy, got a little college but didn't do well there either, got married, got a sales job, and didn't sell anything for two and a half years. And then P. C. Merrell, a leader in his company whom he respected, gave him some advice that changed his life: *"Believe in yourself and go to work on a regular schedule."*

As Dad told his story, I could sense a shift in the room and imagine the thoughts of the people: *Wow, he had it pretty tough growing up, and he overcame some real challenges. You know, if he can, maybe I can too.* This is the concept of identity.

Because people identified with Dad, they were more likely to follow through and take his advice. I bet it's the same for you. Even though an expert tells you what you should do, if you don't have anything in common, you are unlikely to take the expert's advice. However, if that same expert tells you how he overcame the same problem you have and tells you how much that problem impacted his life and the struggle he went through, you are much more likely to take the expert's advice. Why? Because *if it worked for him, and he is just like me, then I bet it will work for me.*

INTENTIONAL CHOICES CHANGE EVERYTHING WHEN IT COMES TO FAMILY

....

If we could teach our kids one thing, it would be the discipline of creating winning habits.

....

I believe the habit of intentionality is critical when it comes to family. When we are intentional, it takes our influence and our example to the next level.

Dad and I enjoyed playing golf on a regular basis. We had a routine where I would pick him up and load his extremely large and heavy golf bag into my car, and we would go to the golf course. After the round I would take him home and unload the golf bag back into his garage.

Even though the day I'm about to describe took place more than twenty-five years ago, I remember it like it was yesterday. We had just finished a great game together, and I was dropping him off. It was a warm summer evening, about eight o'clock, with about forty-five minutes of sunlight left in the day. The temperature was starting to fall into the comfortable low-nineties. In my mind I can hear the birds singing and the locusts calling.

I got out of the car and unloaded his golf bag into the garage, and then we hugged and said good-bye as we always did. As I turned to head back to the car, I heard his voice. "Son, I have something to tell you." I turned around as he approached. He came up to me and put both hands on my shoulders as he looked into my eyes. "Son, I need to apologize. I don't think I have told you enough how much I love you and how proud I am of you."

That moment is in my heart for eternity.

As far as I was concerned, I had as good a relationship with my dad as any son could have with his father. Yet, because of Dad's intentionality, he took it to another level. Even as I write this memory, tears are in my eyes. We had another long hug after those words and then I went home—changed forever.

The choices we make and the actions we take create the habits that create our future. One of the intentional habits I learned from Dad was the habit of taking your kids to as many appropriate business functions as possible. From an early age I traveled with my parents to hear Dad speak at corporate functions and large public events. Because of this, I was exposed to the most influential thought leaders and executives of our times. I have listened to and met Paul Harvey, Norman Vincent Peale, Colin Powell, Steve Forbes, Brian Tracy, Jim Rohn, Denis Waitley, Tom Hopkins, and countless other speakers and celebrities. Mom and Dad knew meeting these people in the right settings would have an impact on me.

Because legacy is a transference of habit, I have done the same thing with my daughter, Alexandra, and she has traveled with me on many business trips. On one of these trips, Alexandra's life was impacted forever. I was invited by Steve McKnight to speak at a large real estate investing education conference in Melbourne, Australia. I now consider Steve a good friend and mentor. I had agreed to do the keynote and several breakout sessions for the group, and Howard Partridge was also on the trip and co-teaching the breakout sessions with me.

Alexandra was seventeen, and she was having a great time on the trip as we saw many of the incredible things Australia has to offer. Plus, we were having a lot of fun with Howard's wife, Denise, and their son, Christian. On the afternoon that Howard and I were doing the breakout sessions, Alexandra was sitting in the back of the meeting room, observing. She was excited to be on the trip, but she was looking forward to the real fun that would start after the business meetings concluded.

The first of our three sessions started just after lunch, and I welcomed people to the room. We had about seventy-five business owners and real estate investors, and it was a lively crowd. We had only an hour, so our approach was to ask them what small-business questions they had and then we would answer and train around those. After we took a few questions, Howard turned to me and said, "Tom, I think we should write these questions down on the board. What do you think?" I agreed and then Howard said, "Alexandra, can you come up here and write these questions on the board for us?"

Oh my! I looked at Alexandra in the back row (who had been minding her own business on her smartphone), and she had the classic "deer in the headlights look" as she stood up. She was not happy! Suddenly she put on the "ballerina smile" (the "ballerina smile" means you are smiling even though your toe is broken and bleeding) and walked with twelve years of ballet poise down the middle aisle toward the front of the room. Her eyes locked with mine, and the daddy-daughter stare began. Laser beams were coming out of her eyes as I felt my face begin to melt. She made her way to the front, wrote down the questions beautifully, and sat down after a few minutes.

Immediately after the session was over, she said, "Dad, tell Howard I don't want to write on the board or be called up to the front. I am happy to be here, but don't ask me to do anything in front of the group." I promised I would tell Howard, but as soon as she left, I was intercepted by several people from the session asking me questions. Before I knew it, the second session was starting.

Howard kicked off the second session: "I want to thank you for coming. In this session Tom and I are going to handle your small-business questions on marketing, sales, operations, administration, and leadership, and we will do some training around each of your questions. Alexandra, can you come to the front and write their questions on the board?"

Yikes! Alexandra was really not happy with me now! She got up and put on the ballerina smile again. As she walked to the front, her eyes locked with mine, but this time nuclear warheads were coming out of her eyes! I knew she was unhappy, and I was in trouble because I hadn't told Howard her request.

She did a great job writing on the board and sat down. Once again, immediately after the session, she made me promise I would tell Howard not to call on her for the last session. Once again I promised I would—and once again I got sidetracked by business owners asking me questions. Before I knew it, the third session was starting and I had still not told Howard.

And that's when it happened. Howard started off the third session: "Alexandra, can you come to the front and write on the board?" Howard and I both looked to the back row where Alexandra had been sitting—she wasn't there! Then we saw her get up. She was sitting at the end of the second row right near the front. She popped out of her seat with a big smile on her face and started writing on the board!

Here is what happened. At each break these awesome Aussies were coming up to Alexandra, asking her questions. "Do you like Australia? Do you travel much with your dad? Where are you going to go to college? Do you think you might be a speaker someday like your dad?" The more questions they asked her, the more she felt like she belonged, the more she felt like an adult. I watched my somewhat shy and reserved seventeen-year-old girl turn into a confident seventeen-year-old woman right before my eyes.

Dad's quote sums it up: "To a child, love is spelled T-I-M-E." Because I had learned this habit from my dad, Alexandra came on this trip and many more. Because of this time we were spending together in different situations, she knew she was loved. Because the people she met thought she could do more than she thought she could—she did!

Be intentional about spending time with your children and

including them in your business and adult situations whenever possible—they will surprise and delight you!

The rest of the story with Alexandra is still unfolding. She has now graduated from college and has her first job. She is working for Howard Partridge, and he is still stretching her outside of her comfort zone.

Being intentional sets you and your family up to win. You can live to win, and living to win starts with the choice to be intentional with those you love and care about most.

One of the things I love is teaching families how to be intentional about their legacies. I recommend that families decide what they want to be known for. Here is a question for you: What do you want other people to say about your family behind your back? What are the words that you want to describe your family's legacy? Here are the words the Ziglar family is known for:

- Hope
- Encouragement
- Character
- Integrity
- Persistent consistency (work ethic)
- Faith

I shared this concept at one of our small-business-owner conferences, and the Hallas family took it to heart and created their own family words around their last name. They shared with me at a following conference what they had done, and I asked if they would send me a letter of what they did and how they did it.

Hi Tom,

It is hard to express in words how we have been impacted by you and your dad. You have been a blessing to us, and we would be honored to be included in your book.

The acronym for our name, Hallas:

Hard working
Adding value
Loving the Lord
Living joyfully
Applying knowledge
Serving others

We were inspired by three people.

One was Mark Timm. We heard him on the *True Performance* podcast and then again at Howard's conference. He talked about having a mission for your family.

The next was Dave Ramsey, who taught his daughters what it meant to be a "Ramsey Girl."

The third person who inspired us was you during your talks about legacy and having one that was worth remembering. You talked about choosing the words that our children's children would be telling each other and discussing those words at the supper table, etc.

To implement what we were learning, we asked our children to think of words that our family should stand for. Later we held a meeting where everyone shared their words, which were written on a dry-erase board by our oldest daughter. We discussed the meanings of the words and voted on the six words that we thought were the best. We chose six because more than that would be too many to remember.

The original phrases were working hard, adding value, learning, attitude of gratitude, wisdom, and serving others. As we were writing down the words that we chose, Jamie realized if we tweaked the way we said them, each word could begin with a letter of our last name, which also just happens to be six letters. Working hard was changed to hard working. Wisdom was changed to applying knowledge. Attitude of gratitude was changed to living joyfully. We also realized that our love for the Lord was not expressed in our family values, so we voted on changing "learning" to "loving the Lord." Having each value begin with a letter of our last name made it easier for our children, for all of us, to remember them.

Now we are in the process of discussing the values we have chosen, what they mean, and how we can live them out, as well as finding Bible verses that support the reason they were chosen.

We thought you might enjoy knowing in our children's words what this process of choosing our legacy means to them, so we asked them to write it down. Here is what they wrote:

Erustus (12): When we did the process of choosing a family legacy, I was excited. It was a bit interesting because we had not done anything like it before. Knowing what a Hallas stands for gives me almost an extra meaning for life. Having a family legacy helps me make decisions up to family standards.

Torah (10): I felt great about having a family legacy. It makes me want to do what a Hallas stands for and helps me want to do what is right.

Isaiah (7): Question: How did you feel going through the process of choosing a family legacy? Answer: It felt fun because we haven't done something like it.

Question: How does having a legacy that we discuss together as a family help you? Answer: So that we know what to do.

Question: Is there anything else you want to share with Mr. Ziglar? (He wrote:) Working harder than before.

Faith (5): I like when we say "I am born to win . . . and I am phenomenal . . ." and what a Hallas is because I think it is great and good to know.

It is helpful because it helps me obey God. I feel great about it.

If you have any questions or need any clarification, feel free to contact us.

May you continue to grow in the grace and knowledge of our Lord and Savior Jesus Christ and continue to encourage and inspire many!
Nick and Jamie Hallas

As you can see, the Hallas family is choosing to win intentionally because they understand it's a choice!

LEAVE INTENTIONAL MARKERS

Mom and Dad decided to move into a senior living community soon after they hit their eighties, and we found a beautiful place only a couple of miles from their home. As we were preparing to move them, it became my job to help clean out Dad's library of more than three thousand books. It was a big challenge: we could keep only a couple hundred books, so which ones would we keep?

I began to go through the books one by one. I noticed that Dad had multiple copies of some, and I knew these were books he kept on hand to give away. I kept one of each of these. As I began to turn the pages in the books, I noticed that Dad had made notes in about every fifteenth book. I started to dig in, and as I was reading one of the books, I could see where Dad had gathered some of his information, and I could tell by the notes in the margin how this information became part of one of his presentations. I could actually see Dad's thought processes on the page, combining what he already knew with this new information. It was like discovering buried treasure!

I closed the book, realizing I had just been given an enormous gift. That is when I discovered the title of the book: *Buried Treasure: Secrets for Living from the Lord's Language* by Rabbi Daniel Lapin. It was as if God spoke to me that my dad had left me markers, and I needed to do the same. I have since reached out to Rabbi Lapin and we have become good friends. I consider him one of my mentors, and he told me that everyone needs a rabbi—even Christians!—so I claim him as my rabbi. Now, when I am reading a good book, I leave markers as well—not just notes for me, but for my daughter and wife, and grandchildren yet to be born. Leaving a legacy by design is about the intentional choices that we make.

Why don't you leave some markers right now? As you read this book, make notes in the margin about what it means to you. If one of your family members comes to mind, write a note to them right on the page. If you are reading this as an electronic version and you are getting a lot out of it, consider getting a paper version as well and reread it, making "love notes" to your family in it. Create a special place in your home for the books that have impacted you the most and write notes throughout the books to those you love. These markers will ripple through eternity.

BE AN INTENTIONAL NOTICER

When it comes to your spouse, your kids, and your grandkids, are you making the daily choice to notice them? I mean really notice them.

If you have an old family photo album, I challenge you to look at pictures taken in 2005 and earlier. Do you have any pictures of young girls between the ages of twelve and sixteen just hanging out? What do you see? Notice the hair, the clothes, the makeup. If they are just hanging out, you will likely see hair in ponytails, T-shirts, jeans, and very little makeup. Now compare this to girls today of the same age just hanging out. What do you notice? Perfect hair, perfect makeup, nice clothes.

Why the change? Now selfies and social media rule and you had better be "broadcast" ready. No longer can you just be yourself; you have to put on the mask and present the image you believe everyone else wants to see and what you believe everyone else's life is really like. No wonder our kids are having such a difficult time.

It's Time to Take Notice!

One of my friends shared this experience with me. He was helping to chaperone a church lock-in for a group of junior high school students. The lock-in would be from six o'clock Friday night until ten o'clock Saturday morning in the church gym. As he was sitting at the front of the gym checking in the kids, he noticed one of the kids walk by, headed straight to the locker room. What he saw shocked him.

A thirteen-year-old girl had on three-inch-high spike heels, an extremely short mini-skirt, a revealing halter top with her midsection exposed, tons of very adult makeup, and her hair done up as if for the nightclub scene. He knew her as a sweet young girl, and he had never imagined this side of her.

Ten minutes later, this same girl came out of the locker room completely changed. All the makeup was gone and her hair was pulled back. She had on sweatpants and a T-shirt and a big smile. He called her over to his table.

"What just happened with the clothes?" he asked.

"I was just seeing if my dad would notice me when I walked by him on the way out."

Ouch. Dads and moms—but especially dads—it's time we notice.

CHOOSE THE RIGHT BOUNDARIES

I love this quote by G. K. Chesterton: "Don't ever take a fence down until you learn the reason it was put up."

It reminds me of the story of the rich lady interviewing chauffeurs. She wanted a good, safe, and skilled driver. She asked each potential chauffeur the same question during the interview: "Would you be fine with driving sixty miles an hour right next to the edge of a cliff?" One after another, they gave her the same answer: "Absolutely! I have had the best training and I am highly skilled." Finally, she asked an older chauffeur the question and his reply was, "Why would you want to drive fast next to a dangerous cliff? I would stay as far away from danger as possible." She hired him on the spot!

Our culture is all about hacking down fences and driving fast next to the edge of cliffs. The fact is, most fences are built for a reason, and it's hard to fall off a cliff if you keep your distance.

What boundaries, fences, do you have in your life? Dad made a decision that Mom was his number one account and he would do nothing to ever cause her concern regarding his relationship to her. Because of this, he decided he would never be alone with a woman other than Mom for any reason. This included being picked up from the airport on his many trips, meetings in his office (door always open), and other professional environments as well. He built the fence far away from the edge of the cliff. The fence may seem silly to some people, but when you see the bodies at the bottom of the cliff, it doesn't seem so silly after all.

What about you? What fences can you build around yourself and around your family?

CHOOSE TO CREATE THE RIGHT ENVIRONMENT

We were having a training class and the subject of marriage came up. My sister Julie was speaking, and her husband, Jim, was in the room. Julie travels the country speaking to nonprofit groups, and her schedule was keeping her on the road. One of the class participants asked this question: "Jim, how do you deal with all Julie's travel and the time you are apart? Isn't it hard?"

Jim's answer was one of the best I have ever heard, and it was one born out of struggle and overcoming the difficult early years of their marriage, which is detailed in Julie's book *Growing Up Ziglar*.

Jim said: "Once I realized that my role as the husband was to create the environment that would allow my wife to become all that God created her to be, everything in our marriage changed."

Wow! The thing I love about Jim's simple response is that you can easily reverse it and say it this way: the role of the wife is to create the environment that will allow her husband to become all that God created him to be.

Imagine a marriage in which both partners are committed to this simple approach. When both partners are committed to this, everyone wins and legacies are created. Having a family that wins truly is a choice. You can intentionally choose habits that will ripple through eternity. Time to take action!

Take a few minutes and do what the Hallas family did. Think about what you want your family to be known for and use the letters of your last name to form the acrostic so it's easy to remember and uniquely yours.

The fastest way to success is to replace bad habits with good habits.
Get your pen out—it's time to take action!

THREE QUESTIONS TO TRANSFORMATION

I want you to write down the answers to these questions in your journal. Clarity helps you make the right choices and take the right actions!

1. What are my desires, dreams, and goals for my family life? (Desire)
2. How will my life be better in the family area when I choose to set the right example and be the right influence in the conversations, actions, and choices I make regarding my family so I can have the family relationships that God created me to have? (Hope)

3. How can I apply grit to my gifts, talents, skills, and experience in the family area of my life? (Grit)

Now it's time to develop the strategy and take action!

Step 1: Identify the Bad Family Habits You Have

What bad family habits are limiting the depth of your relationships with your family members? I am a big believer in "adoption," so don't hesitate to "adopt" others into your family and apply these ideas to them as well. What distractions, technologies, and realities have created bad habits and choices that are holding your family relationships back, that are negative and keeping you from achieving your desires, dreams, and goals?

Write them down in your journal and be specific.

Step 2: Identify the Good Family Habits You Need

What input can you purposefully put into your mind, and what actions can you take that will strengthen the qualities you want to develop in yourself that will allow you to have the influence and example you need to achieve your desires, dreams, and goals faster (for example, education, online courses, positive relationships, such as mentors or coaches, books, podcasts, self-talk, actions you can take, and prioritizing time)?

List them in your journal and be specific.

Step 3: Choose to Replace a Bad Family Habit with a Good Family Habit

Pick a bad habit you want to replace with a good habit. Start small and build up. The key is starting and sticking with it! Each week you build on the same change from the previous week and/or replace another bad habit with a good habit.

Example: In the family area of your life, you identify the bad habit of not prioritizing your family's needs over everything else. The result is there is no intentional time for what really matters: the relationships you have with those you love the most. This creates strained relationships and doubts with your kids, your spouse, and everyone you call family. You determine that life has become so hectic that your time and attention are far too focused on getting the next thing done rather than on building the relationships right in front of you. You decide right now to put family first, and this simple yet profound choice is the decision that will ripple through eternity and create the legacy you want.

Bad family habit: family is not my priority.

Good family habit: daily intentional engagement with my family.

....

*"The words we say to our children today will be
the whispers they hear when we are gone."*

—RODNEY EILAND

....

Here are four examples of how you can make small choices that will transform your life.

Example 1: Every day write a note or send a text to each of your children that tells them you are thinking of them, love them, and are proud of them. Do this every day for sixty-six days until it becomes a habit.

Example 2: Prioritize and set aside a time on your calendar each week for an intentional family discussion around a subject that will matter thirty years from now. The discussion needs to be only ten minutes, and it can happen at dinner, on the phone, or while you are taking a walk. What matters is to intentionally plan to have the discussion and then have it. Do this each week.

Example 3: Ask each person in your family to tell you what matters most to them about your family. Keep notes in your journal and really listen to understand where each person is regarding their engagement to your family. Ask at least one person a day until you know what everyone is thinking and feeling. It's okay to have multiple conversations with each person and then use the "tell me more" question when they start to open up about an issue or area—and listen to their answer. Example: "John, I know you really want to go to the beach for our family vacation. Can you tell me more about why you like the beach?"

Example 4: Identify the words, principles, and values you want your family to be known for and make them part of your family's vocabulary and way of life. These words will become your legacy. Have weekly discussions about these concepts.

Choose to win! Time to take action. Write down in your journal what you are going to intentionally do.

- Bad family habits you are going to get rid of
- Good family habits you are going to implement
- Daily action plan to implement at least one good family habit

This may not seem like much, as it usually takes only a few minutes a day to implement a small good family choice, but when you add to this every week, before you know it your life will be completely changed!

Can you feel it? Hope is rising because you are starting to get clarity on where you want to go, and you have identified the choices you need to make to get there! Your balloon is starting to take flight and gain some altitude, and your family is beginning to enjoy the ride.

Chapter 9

·············

FINANCIAL

Choose to Hope and Dream

> **CHOICE 5:** Making wise *financial* choices inspires your hope and builds your dreams.

One of the things that amazes me is how many people have the wrong attitudes and beliefs about money. A few years ago I posted this quote on our Zig Ziglar Facebook page:

·············

"Money is not the most important thing, but it is relatively close to oxygen."

—ZIG ZIGLAR

·············

Almost immediately a lady posted this response: "I knew Zig Ziglar was all about the money."

That's when the fun began! At that time we had about 2.5 million Facebook fans (now we have close to 5 million). One of the great things about our Facebook fans is that they will come to our defense. I watched the comment section in real time as people began to respond to her comment.

"Have you ever read one of Zig Ziglar's books?"

"Have you ever heard him speak?"

"Why don't you google Zig Ziglar and see what he believes and stands for?"

It was truly awesome as people defended Dad and our philosophy in a loving way. I decided to do a little bit of snooping and checked out the Facebook page of the lady who had made the comment. Believe it or not, the last post on her page said this: "My greatest joy in life is helping those who can't help themselves."

Wow. I agreed with her 100 percent, and then I asked the obvious question: "How can you help someone else if you don't have anything to give?"

I took a break from Facebook and came back a few hours later to see how the responses to her post were going. To my delight, the lady had posted an updated comment. Here is what she said: "Thank you, everyone, for your comments on my post. I researched Zig Ziglar and you guys are right, he is the real deal. Forgive me for my initial response."

Wow! This is proof that good does occasionally happen on Facebook comments. I believe the reason she changed her tune was because of the love and the tone of the comments that our fans made toward her. They understood that she just didn't know what she didn't know.

What beliefs and attitudes do you have about money and your

finances? In your *Choose to Win* life, I want to encourage you to make two choices about how you view money.

Choose to believe:

- It's morally good to earn money.
- It's morally good to make wise financial decisions.

I love what my friend and mentor Rabbi Daniel Lapin says about earning money: "When you solve a problem for someone you are often rewarded with a certificate of appreciation—we call this money. The more problems you solve, the more certificates of appreciation you get. God is never happier with His children than when they are solving the problems of His other children."[1]

God has given you unique gifts, talents, skills, and experiences, and when you use these to solve the problems of His other children, God is well pleased with you! This is good news. Money is simply the fruit, the certificate of appreciation, that rewards you for solving the problems of other people. Money earned in service to others and solving their problems is a very good thing.

When you earn money, you have the moral responsibility to use it wisely. How you handle your finances is key, as you have the moral responsibility to provide for yourself and your family and those God calls you to help.

How are you doing financially? Are you in debt? Are you actively saving for your retirement? Are you living on the edge, where one unexpected expense would create havoc in your life?

I have good news for you. You have a choice! It's never too late to get started or start over again. You can begin today, right now, to begin creating the financial future you want. Here is better news for you: making wise financial choices inspires your hope and builds your dreams.

DREAM OR DISASTER?

I have noticed something in my travels and meeting tens of thousands of people. Most people do not get serious about their financial situation until they encounter what I call the two Ds: dreams and disasters.

Are you closer to your financial *dream* or your financial *disaster*? Getting your financial house in order will determine how much time and how much money you will have to pursue your dreams. Replacing bad habits with good habits creates financial success and gives you the ability to have time flexibility and money to apply to your dreams.

Below is a list of the most common bad habits and financial mistakes people make. These bad habits are eliminated only when they are identified and then replaced with a good habit. In your journal, write a list numbered 1a, 1 to 18 and next to each one, put a yes or no to indicate if you are making that mistake.

Bad Habit 1a: Are you going through life without a clearly identified *why* and a dream? Surprisingly, when I did the research on common financial mistakes, none of the institutional "experts" listed this as a key to financial success. The bottom line is you need a big *why* and a dream so vivid that when temptation comes, you can resist it. Identifying and reviewing your big *why* and your dreams is one of the best habits you can create.

Bad Habit 1: Do you engage in excessive, impulsive, or unnecessary spending? This is the opposite of the greatest wealth-building discipline you have: delayed gratification. The habit of sticking to your budget and saying no to the impulse purchase will help you create the life you deserve.

Bad Habit 2: Do you have never-ending credit card payments? How many payments do you have? How often do you make just the minimum payment? Paying interest on last year's debt is a killer.

Bad Habit 3: Are you living on borrowed money? Home equity loans are just one of the ways you can borrow your way into a "better" short-term lifestyle and a long-term mess.

Bad Habit 4: Do you buy new cars? The average new car loses 60 percent of its value in the first five years. On a $30,000 new car, that is $18,000 flushed down the toilet!

Bad Habit 5: Did you buy too much house? "House poor" is all too common. Make sure you can put down at least 20 percent on your home and do not have to carry PMI. Your house payment should not be more than one-third of your take-home pay.

Bad Habit 6: Do you treat your home equity like a piggy bank? Don't fall into the trap of borrowing against your home for the home improvement or the credit card consolidation loan, no matter how good the numbers seem.

Bad Habit 7: Are you living paycheck to paycheck? As Dave Ramsey says, when you have no savings, Murphy will move into your guest bedroom! Have a garage sale; deliver some pizzas; do whatever it takes to get an emergency fund in place and save some money from each paycheck.

Bad Habit 8: Are you currently making an income but not saving for retirement? Create a budget where you live on 80 percent of your take-home pay and set aside the remaining 20 percent for saving and giving.

Bad Habit 9: Do you have financial debt other than your home mortgage and no written game plan for getting out of debt? How different would your life be if you had zero debt? Would you sleep better? Would you have more peace of mind? Would your dream become a reality sooner? You have a choice to make this happen ASAP—what's your plan?

Bad Habit 10: Did you fail to do the math before you took out student loans? Student loans are far too easy to get and seldom make financial sense. Cash flow in college may mean a little bit of sacrifice in the short run, but can you really justify $50,000 in debt to get a $40,000-a-year job?

Bad Habit 11: Are you living your life without a written budget?

Your money will disappear almost instantly if it doesn't know where it belongs and it makes friends with your credit cards. Remember, budgets make your dreams come true *faster*.

Bad Habit 12: Are you hoping that nothing goes wrong because you have no emergency savings? Don't let a car repair or a trip to the emergency room turn your life upside down. Have some available cash handy, $1,000 minimum. Three to six months' living expenses is ideal.

Bad Habit 13: Did you cosign a loan without understanding that you are on the hook for the loan if the other person can't pay? The bank wants you as a cosigner because they know the main borrower may default, meaning *you* get to pay it. (Banks are smart and have a ton of experience, so if they won't loan money to someone, why would you?)

Bad Habit 14: Do you have a car payment right now? Is your car payment keeping you from reaching your other financial goals as fast as possible? What if you took that car payment and applied it to your big goals and dreams? How much faster would you get your dream house? Your retirement, and so forth?

Bad Habit 15: Are you living without a will, especially if you have minor children? If you don't have a will, have one drawn up now. Living to win is a choice, and few things prevent more problems and tell our children we love them more than preparing for their future in the event of tragedy.

Bad Habit 16: Are you living without adequate life insurance if you have minor children? For the vast majority of people, term-life insurance is extremely affordable and will take care of your family if something happens to you. Ten times your yearly income is a good rule of thumb and will allow your kids to have the same standard of living and allow them to go to college if the money is invested wisely.

Bad Habit 17: Are you living without long-term disability insurance? Statistically, you have a one-in-three chance of needing long-term disability insurance, so be prepared.

Bad Habit 18: Are you living week to week without a financial game plan for your future? Bad Habit 1a was not having a *why* or a big dream. Now you need a financial plan to make your *why* and your dream a reality. Winning financially starts with a choice followed by action.

Unfortunately, I believe the majority of people do not get serious about their financial futures until they are in the middle of a crisis and facing disaster. They live paycheck to paycheck with credit card debt, a mortgage, student loans, car payments, no savings account, no budget, and then disaster strikes. Do any of these disasters ring a bell with you?

- Loss of job
- Unexpected medical expense
- Economy slows down
- Car accident

Now life gets serious. The fun goes out the window. Payments are missed, the phone starts to ring, and before you know it, your car is repossessed and you can't even get to the part-time job you took after you lost your good job. If it hasn't happened to you, I bet you know someone who has had it happen. It's not pretty.

When you are in a financial crisis with nowhere to turn, you suddenly learn the difference between needs and wants. You learn about budgets and you get laser-focused on priorities.

MY OWN DISASTER WITH A CAPITAL *D*

Back in 1998, I came up with what I thought was a brilliant idea. I was thirty-three at the time and had been president of Ziglar for three years. I came up with the idea to start a new business under the Ziglar brand. Dad had a huge following in network marketing circles, and I believed we could significantly grow our company and our reach if we started our own network marketing company to spread the Ziglar philosophy and products.

I took the idea to Dad, and he loved it and supported it 100 percent. It was now my job to create the business plan and launch the new company. We spared no expense and invested more than $250,000 in industry consultants. They all agreed it could be a huge success. Only one industry expert advised us to take it slow and stick with our core. The rest thought our biggest risk would be not to be able to scale fast enough. I fell in love with the numbers and decided to go all in. We invested in new office space, tons of inventory, and a custom computer software for handling orders and commissions, we hired new people, and the list goes on and on.

We launched in 1999 and shut it down less than a year later with *two million five hundred thousand dollars* in debt. For a good many months, I went to bed every night with this thought on my mind: *It took Dad his whole life to build his reputation, and I have destroyed it in less than a year.* I thought it was the end of the world.

During this time, Dad never wavered or worried. Over and over again, Dad told me it would be all right. He believed it, but I didn't. In my mind I was a Failure with a capital *F.* My family supported me. Even the three thousand distributors I had to tell we were closing the business supported me. A few were very upset, and I didn't blame them. I was upset and had lost money, just as many of them had. Those were very dark days.

For months I would go to the office, close my door, and answer calls from the people we owed money. Not fun. I had the honor of missing many paychecks and personal savings began to be used on things like car payments and food.

And then God did what God does. People like Larry Carpenter stepped up and helped us with our short-term financial needs. Dr. Clifton Jolley, the one industry consultant who advised me to "take it slow and stick to your core," helped broker a deal with Nikken, one of the top network marketing companies in the world. Dad became the spokesperson for Nikken, and we found a home for our distributors with them as well.

The spokesperson agreement was big—one million dollars for five years—and Nikken agreed to pay it up front. The check from Nikken came the same week I got a call from the bank. Dad had personally guaranteed the bank loans with his retirement accounts. The market had recently had a big downturn and the accounts were no longer big enough to make the bank feel secure, so they demanded Dad cash out one million to give to the bank in case the markets went down further.

When I think back to this time in my life, I see God's hand in so many ways. I had made incredibly unwise business decisions, and yet God provided exactly what we needed at the exact time we needed it. I thought the Nikken deal was going to give us breathing room to get our core business back on track. Instead, it literally saved my dad's financial future.

The pressure was still on, but in one move we wiped out a million in debt with the Nikken payment to the bank. Every day became the grind of making one small good business decision after another. On a regular basis I was still beating myself up for the situation. I remember a candid talk with my best friend, who walked through this with me. One day on the way home I got a call on my cell phone from Bruce. He asked me how I was doing, and I was blunt with him: "Not good." The pressure was immense, and I was doing everything I could to save Dad's reputation and get out of debt.

What Bruce said to me changed my life: "Tom, have you done everything today you possibly could have done to solve the problems of the company?" I answered with a yes. I was taking all the hard calls, being truthful, and doing everything I could—one little positive baby step at a time.

Then Bruce said: "Tom, when you get home, leave it all outside. You have done everything God expects. You have given it 100 percent and made good decisions all day. Sleep well tonight knowing you did your best and did everything you could. Tomorrow when you get up, do the exact same thing. One day at a time, one good decision at a time. God knows, and He has you covered."

Every time the pressure built back up I replayed Bruce's words in my mind. Whenever I gave Dad an update, his response was always the same: "Keep at it, son. Good job. Everything is going to be okay. God has big plans for us." My family, my friends, and my God all had my back. I still got to sit in the fire I built, but the glaze it created looks pretty good now.

My disaster changed my entire perspective on finances, both in our business and at home. I tasted the reality of massive debt. I now understood budgets, risk, cash flow, and lost opportunities because of bad business decisions. When it came to financial experts, my hearing improved greatly as well. I became a huge Dave Ramsey fan and started applying his teachings to our business. Wow. What a difference!

And Dad was right. Everything was okay. We paid off the debt. Our reputation was maintained. Many of our vendors worked with us. They wanted us to win. It's hard for me to believe that was twenty years ago. It seems like yesterday.

Here is what I learned . . .

- If I had listened to Clifton, we would not have gone into massive debt.
- If I had listened to Clifton, we would not have risked a great business on the new business.
- If I had known about Dave Ramsey and listened to him, well, the list is too long to write!

What about you? Have you had your own financial disaster? Did it help you get your finances in order?

I love this saying:

Fools never learn from their mistakes.

Normal people learn from their own mistakes.

Wise people learn from others' mistakes.

I recommend you learn from my mistakes. Be wise—it's a lot less painful!

GOOD FINANCIAL HABITS

If you are a Dave Ramsey fan, I am sure you can see his influence on me. We have already covered the bad financial habits many people have, and now I would like to share what I believe are the good financial habits you need to build a solid foundation and get out of debt.

Good Habit 1: Input sound financial wisdom into your mind. Listen to, read, and get mentored by wise financial experts who have long track records of success.

Good Habit 2: Get clarity on your big *why*, your dreams and your goals, and write them out in detail. And include a financial plan to achieve them.

Good Habit 3: Create a budget and review it every week until it becomes second nature.

Good Habit 4: Take control of your money one step at a time. Stop digging the hole! Once you have your budget, do whatever it takes to establish a $1,000 emergency fund. No more debt—pay cash for everything as you go. Start paying off your debts, smallest to largest, until you are debt-free except for your house, and then build up liquid savings until you have three to six months of living expenses. Now you are ready to start saving and investing for your retirement. If this approach sounds familiar, it's because I have heard it from Dave Ramsey at least one thousand times!

Good Habit 5: Get solution focused, not problem focused. One of the challenges of being in a financial mess is that feeling of hopelessness when it seems that no matter what you do, it just doesn't matter. Being overwhelmed can be crushing. Remember, you are born to win, and you can choose to win—and it starts with making good, small, and sound financial choices and decisions. Identify solutions and work on them daily, and you will make progress. Note: it's not negative to identify problems; it's only negative if all you dwell on is the problem.

My Dave Ramsey Story

Coming out of my own financial disaster, I was eager to learn good financial principles. Dave Ramsey's books, podcasts, and seminars have been a huge help to me. One of the things Dave teaches is that you should always pay cash rather than lease or finance. I really didn't understand this concept until I saw the numbers for myself.

Years ago, our office manager came to me with some good news. Our copier lease was up, and we could get a new, better copier on a lease for less money. Our lease payments would go down from $1,200 a month to $1,000 a month. My "Dave" radar kicked in.

"How long is the lease?" I asked.

"Thirty-nine months."

"Wow, $39,000 seems like a lot for a copier," I replied.

"Yes, but that includes all the service and maintenance fees, and you know how often copiers break down. Plus, at the end of the lease we can buy our copier from them for only $4,000."

"I am curious, what copier are we getting? Can you give me the brand and the exact model number?"

I went to the internet and in less than a minute I found a copier I could pay cash for and own for less than $13,000.

"Look at this! We can just pay cash for it and save $26,000. Let's do that," I said.

"Okay, but we still need to find out how much service and maintenance will be. I bet it's a lot."

We did our research and got a full-service and maintenance agreement for—get this—$110 a month!

Twenty-six thousand dollars is a lot of money. If I had done what we had always done, I would have signed a new lease and that money would have been lost. My disaster convinced me to seek the right input, which changed my mind-set. A simple, small good habit—let's buy rather than lease—led to huge savings. By the way, eight years later, that same copier is still going strong!

DREAM!

It's time to focus on your dream, especially if you are in the middle of a disaster. Yes, it can be hard to focus on your dreams when you don't know how you are going to make the next car payment, but dreams give you fuel for today and remind you that the sacrifices you are making now are worth it. Why? When you have a compelling dream that guides all your financial decisions, you get the benefit and none of the pain when you apply wisdom—and your hope begins to soar.

....

The hope your dream creates will fuel you
as you grind through your disaster.

....

Getting out of a disaster is usually a grind and is made one good decision at a time. Even if it is a grind, however, you can still choose your attitude as you grow through it. When you understand that every step you take to get out of the mess you are in is also one step closer to your dream, the steps are easier to take! If you have no hope, no dream, or no desire for a better life, then it is unlikely you will take any steps to improve yourself.

"The number one reason people do not reach their goals is they trade what they want most for what they want now."

—ZIG ZIGLAR

You have a choice to make right now. Are you going to plan your financial life on purpose in the context of your dream, in the context of everything you want to be, do, and have? Or are you going to let your financial life just "happen" and hope for the best?

There is a lot at stake when you don't choose to manage your financial life intentionally:

- Your health
- Your marriage
- Your reputation
- Your freedom

Do the dream, not the disaster!

Let's dream a little! Answer the following questions:

- If money were no object, what would you do?
- If you could travel anywhere in the world, where would you go?
- Imagine living in your dream house. What style of house? Where is it? What makes it uniquely yours?
- If you could bless someone or a charity with a financial gift, who would it be? What would you give them, and how would it help them?

Are you ready to start working on your dream? Here are four keys you can use to start identifying and creating your dreams right now.

1. Start before you feel ready.

   Get your pen out and write down in your journal the dreams

you have. It's okay if you aren't sure; the key is to just start! You can add to this later.

2. Break big dreams into smaller steps.

    Example: If your dream is to have a paid-for house and you owe $100,000 on the house, start by breaking it into smaller steps. How much extra can you pay off each month? How can you earn a little bit more or save a little bit more?

3. Get comfortable with being uncomfortable.

    You don't know what you don't know! Review the seven-step goal-setting process in chapter 3 and begin to identify the things you need to learn or do in order to accomplish your dream. A big dream should make you feel uncomfortable. Embrace it and move toward it!

4. Speak and envision your dream into life.

    Make a mental movie of you in the middle of your dream. In your journal write down the dream that you want to work on—write it out big and bold.

    Now write the movie scene description of you in the middle of your dream—lots of detail and lots of emotional and sensory words.

    Example: If your dream is to own your dream home, write a movie-scene script of what you see in your home as you walk from room to room. Include all five senses: what are you seeing, smelling, feeling, hearing, and tasting?

....

"If you aim at nothing, you will hit it every time."

—ZIG ZIGLAR

....

When you have clarity on your dreams—everything you want to be, do, and have—then sticking to a good financial game plan is so much easier. Choosing to win financially is simply replacing bad financial habits with good financial habits.

The fastest way to success is to replace bad habits with good habits. Get your pen out—it's time to take action!

THREE QUESTIONS TO TRANSFORMATION

Write down the answers to the following questions in your journal. Clarity helps you make the right choices and take the right actions.

1. What are my desires, dreams, and goals for my financial life? (Desire)
2. How will my life be better in the financial area when I learn the skills and discipline to make good short-term and long-term financial decisions based on my dreams and not on the need for instant gratification? (Hope)
3. How can I apply grit to my gifts, talents, skills, and experience in the financial area of my life? (Grit)

Now it's time to develop the strategy and take action!

Step 1: Identify Your Bad Financial Habits

What bad financial habits are keeping you from building your financial dream life? Does a lack of financial goals, education, and knowledge, combined with a poor financial mind-set, result in low financial self-discipline that is keeping you from achieving your desires, dreams, and goals?

Write them down in your journal and be specific.

Step 2: Identify the Good Financial Habits You Need

What input can you purposefully put into your mind and what actions can you take that will strengthen the financial skills, attitudes, and beliefs you need to develop that will allow you to achieve your desires, dreams, and goals faster (for example, education, online courses, positive relationships like mentors or coaches, books, podcasts, self-talk, and other actions you can take)?

Write them down in your journal and be specific.

Step 3: Choose to Replace a Bad Financial Habit with a Good Financial Habit

Pick a bad habit you want to replace with a good habit. Start small and build up. The key is starting and sticking with it! Each week you build on the same change from the previous week and replace another bad habit with a good habit.

Example: In the financial area of your life, identify the bad habits of not having specific long-term financial goals and not having a budget or game plan to achieve your goals. Living paycheck to paycheck and wondering if you will ever be able to retire or handle a financial emergency has made any change in the status quo a huge burden. You decide you want to develop the financial skills and beliefs necessary to take control of your financial life so that you can do what you want, when you want, with whom you want!

Bad financial habit: Not having a clearly defined financial goal, budget, or plan.

Good financial habit: Work daily toward my financial goal using a budget and a plan.

Here are four examples of how you can make small choices that will transform your life.

Example 1: Use the Ziglar Goals Setting System in the addendum (p. 213) to create your one-year, five-year, and ten-year financial goals. Work on your financial goals and track them in the Ziglar Performance Planner on a daily basis for sixty-six days, and then as often as necessary to make sure you stay on track.

Example 2: Create a personal budget you review with your spouse (if married) and stick to it. Use a powerful budgeting tool like www.everydollar.com and track every penny you spend as you move toward achieving your financial goals.

Example 3: Choose to get educated in the skills and beliefs necessary to achieve financial freedom. Read or listen to financial experts fifteen minutes a day for sixty-six days until you become skilled and your beliefs about finances allow you to achieve your financial desires and dreams.

Example 4: "Move the needle" short-term and make a huge impact in your behavior and financial position. Create a ninety-day plan to cut every expense, have a garage sale, work for extra income to pay off as much debt as possible, and build a cash emergency fund.

Choose to win! Time to take action. Write down in your journal what you are going to intentionally do.

- Bad financial habits you are going to get rid of
- Good financial habits you are going to implement
- Daily action plan to implement at least one good financial habit

This may not seem like much, as it usually takes only a few minutes a day to implement a small good financial choice, but when you add to this every week, before you know it your life will be completely changed!

Can you feel it? Hope is rising because you are starting to get clarity on where you want to go, and you have identified the choices you need to make to get there. Your balloon is starting to take flight and gain some altitude, and it looks like you are creating some extra spending money to use when you reach your destination.

Chapter 10

PERSONAL

Choose to Use Your Time and Energy Wisely

> **CHOICE 6:** Taking *personal* time gives us the creative energy we need to excel in everything we choose to be and do.

IT'S PERSONAL

Have you ever felt drained? Overwhelmed? Out of gas? One of the keys to creating the future you want is to have the energy you need, the gas in your tank, to deal with life's challenges and achieve your goals at the same time. One of the most common questions I get is, "Tom, how do I stay motivated?" This is a huge challenge! One of the proofs that this is a universal problem is that the bestselling Zig Ziglar audio series of all time at www.ziglar.com is titled "How to Stay Motivated."

Being and staying motivated are key to your success. No matter what your natural disposition is—either generally positive or skeptical, outgoing or introverted—having "pep in your step" allows you to get more done and be more creative in the process.

Good news: taking personal time and creating the habits that give us energy and a more positive outlook are choices all of us can make.

Gooder news: I know *gooder* is not proper English, but every time I say that word it brings a smile to my face! Thanks to my friend Matt Rush for this *gooder* word that gives me energy. When we choose to create habits that give us personal energy, they multiply all the other good habits we are creating.

Yes, it's true what Dad said: "A positive attitude will outperform a negative attitude every time."

I have a question for you: Do you consider yourself reasonably intelligent and possessing at least some common sense? Okay, that was an easy question—of course this describes you. After all, you are reading this book!

Now that we agree you are smart, one of the character qualities of smart people is that they understand the importance of a positive attitude and creating habits that give them energy and the ability to stay positive, even when life gets tough.

....

Attitude is a reflection of character, and
character is a reflection of habit.

....

Tackling life's challenges requires positive creative energy, and positive creative energy requires the right habits. We must have habits that fuel and refuel us daily so that when life knocks us down, we are ready.

Following are twenty choices and habits that will give you energy, allowing you to accomplish more and increase your enjoyment of life. These habits are not "selfish." In fact, they are the opposite of selfish because by regularly working on a few of them, they will give you the energy and creativity you need to solve the problems of more people, and when you solve the problems of other people, you make the world a better place.

1. Choose to Care for Yourself

It is impossible to give something you do not have. Let that thought sink in for a moment. Many people, including me, fall into the trap of helping everyone else without ever taking the time to care for themselves. In order to encourage others, you need a source of encouragement. In order to give others your energy, you have to have energy to give. Choosing to care for yourself is a mind-set and one of the most powerful choices you can make.

As a Christ follower I believe that God will give me the energy to help others when I need it most. I also believe that God expects me to take care of myself so I can serve His other children. The first step in caring for yourself is choosing to make this a priority.

2. Develop a Habitude of Gratitude

What a great phrase! The habitude of gratitude.

Let's break it down. Believe it or not, *habitude* is a real word. It means a custom or habit. Gratitude is a feeling of thankfulness. Habitude of gratitude is another way of saying that we live in a constant state of being thankful rather than being ungrateful, critical, and unappreciative.

....

"Gratitude is the healthiest of all human emotions."

—HANS SELYE, AS QUOTED BY ZIG ZIGLAR

....

It's clear: gratitude is an attitude, and we need to make gratitude a habit. One of the habits I focus on a couple of times a year is what I call the sixty-six days of gratitude. It works like this: Each day for sixty-six days I write down three things I am grateful for without repeating anything already on my list. At the end of sixty-six days I have listed 198 things. That is a long list!

I do this for sixty-six days because that is how long it takes to really cement a habit, according to Gary Keller in *The One Thing*. The habit I am creating is not the habit of writing three things down each day—that is simply the process. I want the habit of always looking for things to be grateful for. Focusing on this for sixty-six days trains my brain to look for the good and to be grateful for even the smallest things.

My dad taught me a lot about gratitude. I will never forget his most powerful lesson on this subject. It was about a year before he passed away, and I was picking him up early one Monday morning to take him to the office for our company devotionals. Dad was struggling with short-term memory loss and Alzheimer's. As we were driving to the office, I remember looking at him and thinking how unfair it was that this great man who had influenced so many lives was going through this. At that very moment, Dad got a grin on his face, slapped the dashboard a couple of times, and said to me, "Son, when I think of my life and all the things God has done for me, my gratitude bucket is overflowing. I have so much to be grateful for!"

Even in the most difficult time of his life, Dad was speaking from his position not his condition. Dad was eternally grateful that he was a child of the King and recognized every day the blessings God had given him. Was that the first time I had heard him express his gratitude? No, I had heard him express his gratitude hundreds of times before. Because he had developed the *habitude of gratitude*, however, he could be grateful in even the most difficult circumstances.

3. Intentionally Learn Something You Can Share That Will Help Someone Else

One way to gain energy and grow is to learn something new that will benefit you. An even better way is to learn something new with the intention of sharing it with someone else so that they can grow. There is something powerful and energizing when your focus shifts to helping others. Helping someone else grow moves you into the significance zone, and there is no greater joy than helping someone else be, do, or have more than they thought possible.

Proverbs 11:25 sums this up perfectly: "Whoever brings blessing will be enriched, and one who waters will himself be watered."

"One who waters will himself be watered." For more than forty years, Dad invested an average of three hours a day learning, reading, and studying life-changing principles and concepts so that he could in turn share them with others. He got watered in the process, and now millions are sitting under the shade of his legacy.

4. Find a Hobby

What hobbies do you enjoy? Golf? Hiking? Knitting? Playing cards? Working with your hands? Hobbies give us energy because they give us something to look forward to and allow our mind and our spirit to rest while we do something we like. This reduces our stress. Many times people stop doing their hobbies because their time is so limited and their stress is so high. If this is you, the thing you have stopped doing is the very thing that can help you break out of your stress and overwhelm cycle.

5. Plan Think Time

Plan time each day to just think. Keep a list of things that require some thought and add to the list as things pop into your mind. Set aside five to ten minutes each day to think about the things that are important and envision the outcome you want. This creates space in your brain when the good idea pops up; instead of losing focus on the project at hand by taking a mental vacation, you can remind yourself that you have your think time scheduled and will handle it then.

6. Plan to Worry

Do you ever get derailed because a worry pops into your mind and you can't let it go? Planning to worry is a good strategy if you are constantly dealing with mental interruptions that are worry related. If this describes you, try this: Plan on a specific time each day to worry—say from 10:00 to 10:10. Then, when a worry pops into your mind, simply tell yourself, *Okay, got it. I will worry about that at ten.*

When you do this, you have instructed your brain that you are going to handle it at a specific time and this frees your brain to think about the next productive thing. The best part about this habit is that when ten o'clock comes, and you go through the things you need to worry about, you will have forgotten half of them and most of the other half will have resolved themselves. Now you can put a plan together to handle the worries that you can take action on. The ones you can't have any effect on, you simply turn over to God.

7. Plan in Advance How You Will Respond to Life's Upsets

One of the best habits you can create and choices you can make is to determine in advance how you will handle life when things go wrong, especially for things you know will eventually happen. For example, if you do a lot of airplane travel, you know that the day is coming when the flight will be delayed or canceled because the weather is bad or the plane is broken. Here is a simple plan you can use to respond rather than react when this happens.

- When you get the news that your flight is canceled or delayed, say out loud, "Fantastic!" This is your key word that says to you that you have got this. Why? Because you have preplanned your response.

- Take comfort in the fact that you have everything in your hands you need to be productive: your phone, your computer, a good book to read, and a beautiful airport to work from.
- Decide in advance you will be stress-free—after all, you can't control the airlines or the weather. Now your only responsibility is to maximize the bonus time waiting for the next flight and find the best next option to get where you need to go.
- Have your airline's customer service numbers handy so you can call them immediately to get your options. You will make this call while you are waiting in the airport line with everyone else who got the same news.

This strategy works for any "upset." Verbally respond positively, remind yourself you have everything you need to be productive, refuse to stress about things beyond your control, and know who to call for help.

Our good friends Jill and Jay Hellwig were on a family vacation when their car broke down in the middle of nowhere over a weekend. This meant they were stuck for three days while a part was shipped in and they would miss their next destination, which they had been looking forward to. They had three young sons at the time, and they decided to treat this change of plans as an adventure and a learning experience. They gathered the boys together and laid out the new plan that went something like this: "Boys, as you know, the car is broken, and it is going to take several days to fix it. This is fantastic! We are now going on an adventure. We will be renting a car for a few days and exploring everything around here." Jill told me it was one of the best vacations they ever had, simply because they decided it would be great.

8. Start Your Day Right

Energy stealers are everywhere. "Emergencies" pop up via text and email as soon as we open our eyes in the morning. One of the best ways to make our lives happen to our days, rather than our days happen to our lives, is to plan time at the beginning of the day to create energy and chart the day. One of the most powerful habits you can form is to start your day with these three vital ingredients: prayer, positive input, and planning. Even if you take only five minutes total to do all three things, it will be the best five-minute investment of your day. I go into detail on this in chapter 12, "The Perfect Start."

9. Write "I Like Because" Notes and Make a Victory List

First you get the email. Then you get the text. Then the phone rings. Suddenly, a series of setbacks has you on your heels and you have lost your mojo. A great way to restore energy is to review your past successes and the kind words that others have said about you. Do you have a victory list? If not, start building one. Review the past goals you have achieved and accomplishments you have made. Write them down on your victory list and keep adding to it. Keep the victory list handy to review on the day when you need a checkup from the neck up!

The "I like because" is another Ziglar concept we have been teaching companies and individuals for more than forty years. The "I like because" is simply a note that recognizes something good someone did. The idea is simple. Whenever you catch someone doing something good, you write them an "I like because" note. Example:

I like Julie because she always notices the little things that others do, and this encourages them and raises the spirits of everyone in the room.

I encourage you to start using "I like because" in your workplace and at home. Whenever you write a sincere, truthful compliment to someone, it brightens their day. Plus, when you save your "I likes" in a special drawer next to your victory list, it gives you the energy boost right when you need it. More than once I have had a particularly tough day, and I will pull out my "I likes" and review some of the notes I have received. We all need to be reminded we have what it takes and that others appreciate us.

10. Text Some Love and Appreciation

I learned this from one of my best friends, Bob Beaudine. In fact, Bob created "Who Friday" from his book *The Power of Who*.[1] You take a few minutes to call or text your friends each Friday to let them know how much you love and appreciate them. When I tried this, I discovered something powerful: I was being lifted up and encouraged in the process. The energy I was giving was nothing compared to the energy I was receiving! Now I choose to call or text some love and appreciation almost every day, and especially when I am feeling a bit down.

Go ahead—test this one right now. Text or call a friend, your mate, or your child and tell them you love and appreciate them and you are thinking about them. This is an amazing habit that will change you and those you love and creates more energy for everyone.

11. Sleep

As we discussed in chapter 7, sleep is more important to our overall health than diet or exercise. Seven hours of sleep each night for almost everyone is the minimum requirement, and if your stress load and workload are high, you definitely need to do everything possible to get your sleep. Reread the tips in chapter 7 to remind you of habits you can start to get better sleep. Along with those suggestions, here are two more tips:

Delay the commitment. Nothing zaps your energy like making one more commitment, especially when you are already drained. Do what Dad did. Dad would say, "If you need an answer right now, it's no, but if you can let me think on it, I can get back to you tomorrow." Review the request the next morning when you have both time and energy to consider it.

Mentally reset—just stop it! Pay attention to your thoughts and make a commitment to stop the negative self-talk. Just saying "Stop it!" can act as a good reset button. While writing this book I decided to lose a few of my extra pounds by eating a very low-carb diet and focusing on whole foods with no processing or chemicals. About ten days in I had lost six pounds and my clothes were already fitting much better, but my self-talk had gone negative and whiney. I was having a pity-party. Here is what I did.

- First, I said to myself, "Stop it!"
- Second, I sat myself in the "corner" and had a good conversation with myself.
- Third, I asked myself these questions:
  - "Have you made good progress in the last ten days?" "Yes."
  - "Have you liked everything you have eaten?" "Yes."
  - "Have you been hungry?" "No."
- Fourth, I made the mental reset and put this in my self-talk, based on a tip from Ziglar Legacy Certified Trainer Steyn Rossouw: "I am getting fitter and fitter every day in every way, and I love never being hungry and eating food I like while losing weight."

12. Make Sure You Are Not Whining to Yourself
Nothing robs your energy like constant whining.

13. Paint a Fence
There is nothing like a project with a beginning and an end that allows you to visibly see the impact you are making. Yard work, painting a fence, and cleaning out the garage are things where we can see our impact and yet we often avoid doing. Now when the pressure

builds and my energy is lagging, I look for a "mindless" job I can do that will allow my mind to wander while my hands work and progress is being made. In fact, one of my most memorable projects was painting our fence—not in the fastest way possible, but in the slowest way possible. I would go out for a few hours at a time and paint one board at a time. The physical activity, the mental think time, and daily progress were exactly what I needed to gain some momentum and create some energy—and make my wife happy! What simple project can you do like painting a fence? Write it down in your journal.

14. Walk in the Woods

One of the greatest ways to increase your energy and peace of mind is to spend time in nature. A walk in the woods or a stroll through a park has numerous benefits, according to an April 22, 2016, *Business Insider* article. Citing numerous scientific studies, the list of benefits includes:

Improved short-term memory
Restored mental energy
Stress relief
Reduced inflammation
Better vision
Improved concentration
Sharper thinking and creativity
Possible anti-cancer effects
Immune system boost
Improved mental health
Reduced risk of early death[2]

Investing in some nature time does wonders for your soul, improves your mood, reduces stress, elevates your focus, and improves your short-term memory. All these benefits give you energy and improve your creativity.

15. Take Short Exercise Breaks

How sedentary is your lifestyle? Do you find yourself stuck at a desk most of the day, with very little movement other than your fingers on your keyboard? This type of lifestyle literally drains the energy and the life out of you. If your goal is to get more joy out of life, have better health, and be more productive and creative in your work and your relationships, then short exercise breaks throughout the day will give you the energy boost you are looking for.

These breaks don't have to be long or intense. The main thing is to stand up, move, and get your blood flowing, your muscles stretching, and your lungs expanding. Plan on setting a timer that gets you up and moving about every sixty to ninety minutes at least four times a day. Add a three-minute walk or a couple of flights of stairs to your bathroom break.

16. Intentionally Daydream

I believe the best time to dream is with your eyes wide open. Creating the *Choose to Win* life is about "seeing" the life you want and then choosing the habits that will create that life. One of the most powerful tools you have is the ability to create the future you want using one of God's most powerful gifts: your imagination.

Try this right now. Imagine it's a year from now and everything in your life is going exactly how you want it. Think about your health, your relationships, your finances, your career, your free time, and your hobbies. Think about where you are, who you are with, and what you are doing. In your mind everything is possible. Enjoy that moment. How does it feel? Creating that future will depend on the choices you make and the habits you build.

My uncle Bernie Lofchick, who was Dad's best friend, shared the following with me:

....

"The most powerful nation in the world is imagiNATION. The weakest nation in the world is procrastiNATION."

....

Go ahead. Daydream. Do it now.

17. Learn a Word a Day

Creativity gives you energy, and energy gives you creativity. One of the simplest ways to boost both your energy and creativity is to learn one new word a day. When you learn a new word, it expands your brain and connects with all the things you already know. New words allow you to better understand things you are working on, and growing your vocabulary allows you to communicate more effectively.

A great resource for learning new words and getting a fresh new perspective on words you already know is *What a Great Word*. In this book, Karen Ann Moore goes deep into the spiritual meaning of words. Appropriately enough, *choices* is one of the 366 words Karen explores in her book:

> One of the ways you continually write and edit the story of your life is through the choices you make. Sometimes you go for the high quality, much sought-after, best parts of life, and other times, you simply choose to move on and not think too much about the consequences. Unfortunately, even when you're weary, even when you decide not to choose, a choice has been made and it often comes with results you did not intend.

Whether we're making vocational choices or emotional or spiritual choices, we have to understand that we are connected to the results. When the outcome is one that satisfies our hearts because we were pleased and excited with the choice we made, then it's a great day. When we make any kind of choice without including our heart as a guide, we can't help but suffer disappointment. The choice is yours each day, but the best choices are attached to your heart.[3]

Learning this not only gives your brain the candy it loves, it also builds your spirit by giving you hope and encouragement. Learning a word a day is a great habit you can choose!

18. Create Your Play List

Music has the power to move your soul. Inspirational and motivational messages give you the push and encouragement you need to power through the tough times.

....

"Music is a moral law. It gives soul to the universe,
wings to the mind, flight to the imagination, and
charm and gaiety to life and to everything."

—PLATO

....

Take some time to create playlists of your favorite songs. Pay attention to the words of the songs and make sure they give you energy, hope, and encouragement. You might want to create several playlists of five to ten songs each designed to help you build attitudes you are working on, like gratitude, hope, and enthusiasm. Keep your motivational and inspirational programs handy as well. Nothing fuels the spirit like listening to a little bit of Zig Ziglar!

If you really want to go the extra mile, I encourage you to record your own voice reading the Ziglar Self-Talk Cards found at the back of this book. This life-changing procedure takes only a few minutes, and it works because you are claiming the Qualities of Success that God has given you. Record yourself reading the affirmations, add it to your play list, and feel your energy grow!

19. Get Out of Town

My good friend David Wright, who has been a coach for more than twenty years and who developed our Ziglar coaching program, shared this quote from Mark Batterson:

....

"Change of place. Change of pace. Change of perspective."

....

Sometimes to achieve a breakthrough and get our energy and creativity up, we just need to get out of town. The change of place and pace gives us the change of perspective we need to see things in a new way.

This book is proof of this concept. This book idea came to me more than four years ago. No real progress came about, however, until I got out of town. I took a road trip with my agent and friend Bruce Barbour, and we went to Albuquerque, New Mexico, and rented an Airbnb house in the Sandia Mountains. In three days we outlined this book and wrote the book proposal—the fact you are reading this is proof that change of place, change of pace, change of perspective works.

20. Putting It All Together—the Power of Multiplication

There are so many things you can do to create energy and creativity in your personal life. Getting and staying motivated is a choice, and to have a lifelong impact, your choices need to become habits.

The good news is your habits and your choices benefit from the power of multiplication. Imagine taking a short walk in a park. On this walk you are listening to the playlist you created that includes your self-talk affirmation recording. You pause to take a cool drink from your water bottle and you reflect on three things you are grateful for. You pull out your stretch band and do sixty seconds of exercise. Before you start walking again, you text a friend that you were thinking about them and that you love them. As you head back to the office, you begin to daydream about how things will be in a year. Wow! In this short walk you improved your personal life and energy nine different ways.

You have what it takes.

The fastest way to success is to replace bad habits with good habits.

Get your pen out—it's time to take action!

THREE QUESTIONS TO TRANSFORMATION

I want you to write down the answers to these questions in your journal. Clarity helps you make the right choices and take the right actions!

1. What are my desires, dreams, and goals for my personal life? (Desire)
2. How will my life be better in the personal area when I create the habits that give me energy and allow my creativity to grow in every area of my life so that I can become the person that God created me to be? (Hope)
3. How can I apply grit to my gifts, talents, skills, and experience in the personal area of my life? (Grit)

Now it's time to develop the strategy and take action!

Step 1: Identify the Bad Personal Habits You Have

What bad personal habits do you have that are creating an unbalanced life and not allowing you to be refueled, therefore limiting your attainment of your desires, dreams, and goals?

Write them down in your journal and be specific.

Step 2: Identify the Good Personal Habits You Need

What input can you purposefully put into your mind and what actions can you take that will strengthen the personal choices you can make that will give you the growth, energy, and creativity you want to develop in yourself? What habits can you develop that will allow you to achieve your desires, dreams, and goals faster (for example, education, online courses, positive relationships like mentors or coaches, books, podcasts, self-talk, actions you can take, hobbies you can work on, and friendships you can nurture)?

Write them down in your journal and be specific.

Step 3: Choose to Replace a Bad Personal Habit with a Good Personal Habit

Pick a bad habit you want to replace with a good habit. Start small and build up. The key is starting and sticking with it! Each week you build on the same change from the previous week and/or replace another bad habit with a good habit.

Example: In the personal area of your life you identify the bad habit of doing everything but taking care of yourself. It seems every second of every day is spent working on a project or helping someone else, and you have no personal time to reflect, refuel, refire, and work on anything that gives you joy just because you want to do it. The result of this is burnout and the belief that you will never be able to do what you want to do. You determine that life has become so hectic that your time and attention are far too focused on getting the next thing done rather than taking care of yourself. You decide you want to develop the personal skills and beliefs to prioritize yourself back into your life because you realize you need energy and creativity to grow to the next level.

Bad personal habit: running out of time every day without ever recharging your creative energy battery.

Good personal habit: schedule regular time to do the things that give you energy and expand your creativity.

Here are four examples of how you can make small choices that will transform your life.

Example 1: Identify ten things that bring you energy and allow you to refocus, relax, and think more clearly. Each day plan time in your schedule to do at least one of these activities with the intent of creating space to be creative and to get filled up.

Example 2: Choose one of the ten things you identified that bring you energy and set a big goal around it. If you get energy from hiking, your big goal could be a three-day hiking trip where you invest the majority of the time hiking in a beautiful place, followed by a good meal and a massage. Set a date for this and make it happen.

Example 3: Investigate something new you have always wanted to do but have never done. Take a course, learn to cook a new type of food, or take up a new hobby. Keep a journal of what you learn and how it makes you feel. Notice if your energy and creativity improve. Track this in your Ziglar Performance Planner.

Example 4: Unplug! Take three days, or more if possible, and disconnect from all technology. Go old-school and use a pen and paper to think about who you want to become. Do this with an uncluttered mind. Set a date and make this happen.

Choose to win! Time to take action. Write down in your journal what you are going to intentionally do.

- Bad personal habits you are going to get rid of.
- Good personal habits you are going to implement.
- Daily action plan to implement at least one good personal habit.

This may not seem like much, as it usually takes only a few minutes a day to implement a small, good personal choice, but when you add to this every week, before you know it your life will be completely changed!

Can you feel it? Hope is rising because you are starting to get clarity on where you want to go, and you have identified the choices you need to make to get there. Your balloon is starting to take flight and gain some altitude, and you are cutting the ropes that have been keeping you tied to the ground!

Chapter 11

....

CAREER

Choose True Performance over Uninspired Inactivity

> **CHOICE 7:** *Career* choices resulting in true
> performance require the right attitude, effort, and skill.

....

"If you do more than you are paid to do, eventually
you will get paid more for what you do."

—ZIG ZIGLAR

....

The seventh spoke of the Wheel of Life is the career spoke, which
is the economic engine that allows you to earn a living and take
care of your financial needs and wants. Whether you are a business

owner, a manager, a teacher, a salesperson, or an investor, how well you perform at what you do determines to a large degree your financial results and even your degree of internal satisfaction and happiness. I understand that everyone's situation is unique, and some circumstances are not necessarily fair or in your control, but no matter what your situation, you have far more to gain than you have to lose by approaching what you do with the right attitude, effort, and skill.

When I was a teenager, Dad took us out to eat at a nice steak restaurant. We sat down, and our waiter brought us the menus and took our drink orders. Right after he left, the busboy came over and started filling our water glasses. He was a young man, not much older than I was. He reached out quickly, grabbed a glass, filled it with water, and set it back down, sloshing water on the table. This happened two more times before Dad asked him a question: "Young man, how are you doing today?"

"Not so good. I don't like my job."

Dad's eyebrows raised. "Don't worry, young man, you won't have it for long."

Wow! I very rarely saw this side of Dad, but he had a knack for reading people. The young man quickly left the table. About two minutes later he came back to the table and spoke to my dad.

"Sir, I want to thank you for pointing out that my attitude was not good. I do like this job. I just had a bad moment, and I wanted to let you know I am back on track and I appreciate that you spoke to me directly. Please accept my apology."

Dad then complimented him for his maturity at recognizing the situation and adjusting his attitude and having the courage to come back and apologize. We had a great dinner, and Dad majorly influenced two people that night: the busboy and me.

Performance, doing a job well, is a combination of attitude, effort, and skill. I have developed a mathematical formula based on this idea that I believe illustrates the power of these three elements. I call it the Ziglar Performance Formula.

$$\text{Attitude} \times \text{Effort} \times \text{Skill} = \text{Performance}$$
$$A \times E \times S = P$$

Have you ever wondered why the top 5 percent in almost every industry will earn four, five, six, even seven times more than the average earner in their industry? The Ziglar Performance Formula will clearly show you why this is the case. Let's take a close look at what each word in the formula represents.

PERFORMANCE

Early in my career at Ziglar I came to a startling realization: Nobody buys training, books, audio programs, or seminars solely for the information they offer. Instead, people are buying the *results*. They believe our materials can help them improve their performance, which, in turn, will improve their results. In fact, I propose that the reason you are still reading this book right now is because you have already gotten—and believe you will get even more—ideas, tips, concepts, and philosophies that will help you improve your performance and get better results in all areas of your life.

No matter what you do to earn money, you are in the problem-solving business, and the better you perform, the more problems you will solve, and the more certificates of appreciation you will get.

About fifteen years ago I took our company through the process of defining what we did as a business. Out of that exercise came the concept that we are in the "True Performance" business—that is, we inspire and help individuals and companies achieve True Performance. As a team, we spent hours discussing what we meant by that term and created this definition: "*True Performance* is the ideal accomplishment of a goal, aspiration, or objective."

I was so proud of this definition that I immediately took it to Dad. I handed him the sheet of paper it was written on and he read it to himself. (I could see his lips moving.) He read it again silently (his lips were still moving). He tilted his head and looked up for a moment and got out his pen. He then added four words that took the definition from good to better than good!

"*True Performance* is the ideal accomplishment of a goal, aspiration, or objective *that benefits everyone involved.*"

With a few strokes of the pen, Dad transformed an idealistic definition into a meaningful and measurable definition. True Performance is when you do the very best job possible and everyone wins. If this sounds vaguely familiar, compare it to the most famous of all Zig Ziglar quotes:

....

"You can have everything in life you want, if you will just help enough other people get what they want."

....

Simply put, when you complete a job, project, or sale, everyone must win in order for it to be considered True Performance. The customer, the salesperson, the support team, the leadership of the company, and the community must all win. There are few things more satisfying in life than solving problems and achieving True Performance in the process.

ATTITUDE

Attitude is the way you think or feel about someone or something. What is your attitude toward your work? Your customer? Your teammates?

It's easy to recognize good attitudes and bad attitudes. Attitudes either bring energy or deplete energy. Nothing moves a relationship or an opportunity faster than attitude. I have walked out of restaurants because of bad attitudes (rude, being ignored), and I have waited for more than an hour in restaurants just to be served because of great attitudes.

....

"A positive attitude will out-perform a negative attitude every time."

—ZIG ZIGLAR

....

EFFORT

Effort is hustle and smarts. Giving 100 percent effort not only means you are working hard and fully focused, but you are also working smart, executing a good plan that is well thought out. My friend Don Sherman was in the FBI and on the Dallas SWAT team. I asked him how they trained to go fast when they practiced for hostage-rescue scenarios. He quickly told me they never trained to go fast—going fast gets you killed. Instead, they trained to go smoothly. Each member on the team works together so they can protect each other and rescue the hostage with the best chance of no one getting hurt. Doing the work is critical, but doing the work the right and smooth way adds years to your life!

SKILL

Skill is the ability to do something well. Great skill comes after learning, training, repetition, and practice. In order to maximize your economic engine, you need great skill, no matter what you choose to do. Professionals understand this and are constantly learning, training, and developing their personal and professional skills.

THE ZIGLAR PERFORMANCE FORMULA

The following is a simple illustration of how the formula works. Do you remember your very first "real" job? Do you remember how you felt on the first day you started? Chances are you were nervous and had a lot of questions, such as:

- Will I fit in?
- Will the people here like me?
- Will I mess up and get fired?
- Will I be able to learn everything fast enough and do a good job?

When you walked in, your attitude may have been a little unsure. Since it was your first day, they had not given you any work to do (your effort), and they had not yet given you any training, which means you had no specific skill yet. This means in the Ziglar Performance Formula your attitude was a 1, your effort was a 1, and your skill was a 1.

$$\text{Attitude} \times \text{Effort} \times \text{Skill} = \text{Performance}$$
$$1 \times 1 \times 1 = 1$$

Walking in, your performance score is 1.

Now imagine as soon as you show up on your first day you meet with your boss and she gives you this speech right out of the gate:

"Thank you for being thirty minutes early. What a great way to start your first day on the job. I want you to know you are going to do fantastic here. You did great in the interview process with each of our team members, and the assessments we did told us that you are perfect for this starting position. I believe that if you bring the right attitude, effort, and skill every single day you will rapidly advance. Our whole team is ready to answer any questions you have. I know this is your very first job, and I want you to know that we are thrilled to have you on the team.

"Here is your schedule for the first day. You will sit with each person on the team, and they will share what they do and how you will be working with them. You will finish the day with HR. They will complete all your official paperwork, get you set up at your work station, and answer any questions. Welcome aboard!"

Wow! It would be amazing if everyone's first day on the job were like this! If this were you, how would you feel? No question about it, your attitude would be more positive and your confidence would be soaring. The right words from your boss moved your attitude from a 1 to a 2.

$$\text{Attitude} \times \text{Effort} \times \text{Skill} = \text{Performance}$$
$$2 \times 1 \times 1 = 2$$

Your attitude improvement alone has doubled your performance. You are what I call "elevator dangerous." Elevator dangerous is simply when you are on an elevator and somebody asks you why you look so happy because you are smiling so big. You answer, "I love my job!" They then ask, "What do you do?" and you reply, "I have no idea! It's my first day and it is awesome!"

The reality is, because you're new to the job, your boss has no fear that you will speak out of turn to one of her customers or prospects. She knows your positive attitude will more than make up for your lack of skills or knowledge and that if you get asked a question you can't answer, you will simply say with a big smile on your face, "I am brand-new here. Let me find someone on our team who can help you."

Since your first day on the job was awesome, you are very excited about the second day. You arrive thirty minutes early again, and as you walk in, one of your teammates says, "The boss wants to see you." Excited, you walk quickly to her office, hoping for another speech. You are not disappointed.

"Wow!" she says. "I think your first day was the best first day any new team member has ever had. Everyone loves you. You asked great questions, your attitude was outstanding, and you are catching on fast. Keep it up! Today I am going to give you some work to do that will introduce you to our customers and help us complete a project. Here is a list of a hundred customers we sent packages to ten days ago. All I need you to do is call and confirm that they received the package. If they say yes, then mark it down on the list. If you leave a voice mail, just let them know to call or email you back if they didn't get the package. And, of course, if they didn't get the package, let them know we will send another one out right away and forward that information over to John so he can handle it. Here is the list of customers and a description of what was in the package, in case they ask. Do you have any questions?"

"No," you reply.

"Great! Keep me posted on how it's going. This is going to help us finish up this project. I am glad you are on the team!"

You go to your desk and start making the calls. One hundred calls never went by so fast. You had energy, your attitude was good, and your effort was great. You already had the skill of making a phone call. On day two your attitude was a 2, your effort was a 2, and your skill was a 1. Your performance doubled again!

Attitude x Effort x Skill = Performance
2 x 2 x 1 = 4

What a great start to your new job. On day three you arrive thirty minutes early again and, just as you had hoped, your boss wants to see you. You hurry down to her office because words of encouragement never get old.

"Amazing! Your first day was fantastic, but your second day was even better! One of our customers actually called me and complimented you on the voice mail you left for her. She said your message was clear and enthusiastic and she appreciated the follow-up and your concern for her. Keep up the good work!

"Today I have another project for you. This project is with our top thirty customers, and I am going to give you some training you need to complete the project. As you know, we provide hardware and software to our key customers. Last month we sent out a software update download via email to our top thirty customers. I need you to call and confirm with each of them that they were able to install the software successfully. This is a fairly easy thing to do, but not everyone is comfortable loading new software onto their computers. Here is a script I want you to internalize and memorize that will allow you to help each customer with the installation if they have not done it yet. The script also covers all the questions you may get and the answers to those questions. Let me know when you feel comfortable with the information and then we can role-play some calls together, and I will let you know when you are ready to start calling."

You go back to your desk and study the script until you know it by heart and then you call your boss, letting her know you are ready to role-play the script with her. After an hour of role-playing with your boss, she enthusiastically lets you know you are ready to make the calls. The thirty calls fly by faster than you imagined. Your attitude is a 2. Your effort is a 2. And now you are using skills specific to your new role, so your skill has moved from a 1 to a 2 as well. Your performance has doubled again!

$$\text{Attitude x Effort x Skill = Performance}$$
$$2 \times 2 \times 2 = 8$$

I love sharing this scenario because it shows us how performance really works. Now I have some good news and some bad news. The bad news is that, in the example above, more than 90 percent of people stop putting their best attitude, effort, and skill forward at this point. They depend on their boss, or their circumstances, or (you fill in the blank) to determine success, but the good news is that some people choose the ownership mentality.

The Ownership Mentality

In order to choose to win, you need to choose the ownership mentality when it comes to your attitude, effort, and skill. In the scenario I gave, your attitude, effort, and skill were positive because you had a great boss. The ownership mentality means you don't depend on your boss, or anyone else, for your attitude, effort, and skill.

You own it!

You own your attitude. You don't care what kind of mood the boss is in. You don't care about the traffic or the weather. You have made the choice to have a fantastic attitude that is positively contagious, and you have created winning habits that keep your attitude positive. Your attitude day in and day out is a 3.

You own your effort. You don't care what the average is. You want to know what the top person in the country is doing when it comes to effort. You always do a little bit extra, and you take time in planning and prioritizing your workday. Your effort day in and day out is a 3.

You own your skill. You appreciate the training your company provides, but you don't stop there. You are always going the extra mile to learn more, and you invest in yourself both personally and professionally. Your skill day in and day out is a 3.

When you apply ownership to the Ziglar Performance Formula, it looks like this:

$$\text{Attitude} \times \text{Effort} \times \text{Skill} = \text{Performance}$$
$$3 \times 3 \times 3 = 27$$

Now you know why the top 5 percent in almost every industry outearn the average earners by so much! They own their attitude, effort, and skill.

Imagine in the scenario example if you had done the following things on top of what your boss suggested:

Attitude: What if each day you had gotten up early to prepare for the day by reading and listening to information both inspirational and educational? What if, on your drive to work, you listened to some great Zig Ziglar programs and called a like-minded friend to encourage him or her and to get encouragement?

Effort: What if, when your boss had given you the calls to make, you planned and organized them in a way to work more efficiently? What if you had asked the boss who on the team had the most experience doing this same type of thing, and you had gone to ask them the best way to approach the calls? What if, when you finished, you had immediately gone back to your boss to ask for more people to call?

Skill: What if, when your boss trained you on the script and the role play, you had also done a little Google search on the best practices for leaving voice mails and making phone contacts? What if you had asked your boss if there was any other information you could relay to the customers while you had them on the phone that might benefit the customers and your business?

As you can see, when you choose to own your attitude, effort, and skill, the possibilities are endless. You can always find ways to create more value and do just a little bit more. It is the addition of the little things that makes the big difference and takes your performance to the next level.

The Massive Impact of a Negative Attitude on Performance

Have you wondered what impact a negative attitude has on performance? It's huge! Let's plug a negative attitude into the Ziglar Performance Formula and see what happens. In a mathematical equation, when you change the value of an integer from positive to negative, the product of the equation goes from positive to negative.

$$\text{Attitude} \times \text{Effort} \times \text{Skill} = \text{Performance}$$
$$-2 \times 2 \times 2 = -8$$

That's right! A negative attitude changes the results from positive to negative. Here is what is even more worrisome. Suppose someone on the team has been there a long time and they have terrific effort and skill, but they have a terrible attitude. Now look at the results:

$$\text{Attitude} \times \text{Effort} \times \text{Skill} = \text{Performance}$$
$$-2 \times 3 \times 3 = -18$$

This type of employee is costing the company a fortune because they are infecting prospects, customers, employees, and vendors with their negative attitude. Many studies have shown that it is cheaper for a company to send a negative employee home with pay than it is to allow them to negatively impact the organization. Does this surprise you? I bet you are thinking of a few examples of this in your own life right now.

Telling people about the Ziglar Performance Formula is one of the most powerful talks I give to corporations because it makes the intangible tangible and demonstrates the real cost of a negative attitude and not having ownership mentality when it comes to performance. The discussion and Q & A around this formula often dramatically impact the performance of the entire organization very quickly, just like it will impact your own performance very quickly.

The Sequence Is Important!

In the Ziglar Performance Formula, we intentionally start with attitude and then move to effort and then skill. Great coaches know this. A great attitude drives effort and skill. For some reason, this sequence is ignored in most businesses and academic institutions. Think about it. Almost every business starts training new hires on their skills first, then they give them work to do (effort), and then when performance is lagging they give them negative attitude incentives. No wonder so few in the marketplace have the ownership mentality.

50 PERFORMANCE HABITS YOU CAN CHOOSE TO OWN

Now it's time to "own" your performance. How do you rate yourself using the Ziglar Performance Formula? Go ahead and rate yourself now:

Attitude x Effort x Skill = Performance

____ x ____ x ____ = _____

The following are fifty performance habits in the areas of attitude, effort, and skill. In your journal write the following headings followed by numbered lists: Attitude Habits (1–11), Effort Habits (12–30), and

Skill Habits (31–50). Please take a personal inventory and rate yourself on each one of the fifty habits by marking a 1, 2, or 3 by the numbered lists.

1 means it is an unrecognized or undeveloped habit.

2 means you have it but tend to do only the minimum required.

3 means you own it and exceed expectations in this area on a regular basis.

Attitude Habits

1. You determine your attitude in advance. You choose to celebrate the good news and embrace the setbacks with an overcoming, can do, positive attitude before the situations happen.

2. You watch your body language. You engage your face, your smile, your demeanor, and your entire body so those around you know you are committed, helpful, listening, and someone they can count on to solve the problem.

3. You are curious. Being curious about someone else and their challenges is one of the greatest and most powerful compliments you can pay. Being ready with questions like, "Can you tell me more about that?" and "How does that impact you?" opens doors and allows you to serve others.

4. You are focused. You determine your primary focus in advance when working on a project or with people and let your attitude and demeanor show your focus.

5. You are 100 percent all in. You are committed! You are all in or consider not doing it at all. You make sure your words, actions, and body language back up the expectations you have set.

6. You act with purpose. You are intentional in your actions, knowing that each thing you do gets you one step closer to your desired outcome. Acting with purpose demonstrates confidence.

7. You are grateful. Each day you take some time to reflect on

the experiences, people, and opportunities that have enriched your life and positioned you to achieve your dreams and goals. Gratitude is the healthiest of all human emotions.

8. You are generous with your time, treasures, and talents. Rabbi Daniel Lapin says, "Opportunity seeks out the generous." People you want to do life with, and who refer business, don't spend much time with misers and Scrooges.

9. You take inventory. At the end of each day you take an attitude inventory: Where did you do well and what can you do better next time?

10. You relish the small stuff. You understand and believe that the many small things done right and with the right attitude give you the best chance for success—and usually don't take much talent or skill. My dad said, "The big shot is just the little shot who kept on shooting."

11. You tell the truth in advance. Even if you don't "feel" like it right now, you decide how you want to feel and speak it as if you already feel that way.

Effort Habits

12. You are early. It's a choice. Make it a habit.

13. You are prepared. You learn in advance everything you can that gives you the best chance for success.

14. You organize and prioritize. You have a plan for your day so that your life happens to your day and not your day happens to your life.

15. You do extra. You exceed expectations so that every interaction you have builds trust.

16. You practice persistent consistency (PC). You work on your big goals every day (consistency) and do just a little bit extra on each goal every day (persistency).

17. You stretch yourself every day. You choose to do at least one

thing each day that is out of your professional comfort zone and takes you into the effectiveness zone.

18. You focus on the process not the results. You take joy in perfecting the process (which you can control) and don't waste energy thinking about the results (which oftentimes you have no control over).

19. You fuel your engine. You maximize your effort by getting enough sleep, eating right, and exercising.

20. You get some vitamin D. In fact, you check your vitamin D levels, which give you fuel to increase your effort. There is nothing like this vitamin, or a little bit of direct sunlight, to boost energy and attitude.

21. You deal with stress. You create a strategy to deal with stress, as stress impacts your potential effort and effectiveness.

22. You don't multitask. You focus on one thing at a time.

23. You manage interruptions. You identify the interruptions you get on a daily basis and have a plan to deal with them. For example, you turn off email notifications so they don't pop up when you are working on a project.

24. You finish strong. Just like your first impression when meeting someone, strongly finishing an interaction or project amplifies the impression and the results of your work.

25. You keep a time log. You know what you are doing and how much time you are spending on each activity in your day. Once you know the situation, simple changes get massive results.

26. You eliminate, simplify, and delegate. What are you spending effort on each day that you can get rid of? Simplify? Delegate?

27. You gamify your performance. What are your IPAs (Income Producing Activities), the things you do each day that directly result in income? If you are in sales, a few examples could include a LinkedIn post, leaving a voice mail message, or having a face-to-face meeting where you give a proposal and ask

for the business. Give each one of these a point value: 1 point for a LinkedIn message, 2 points for a voice mail to a prospect, 20 points for a face-to-face meeting where you give a proposal and ask for the business. Don't finish your day until you have earned 100 points.

28. You immediately take care of tasks that take less than two minutes. Do it now. If it's something you have to do, and it comes up, you do it now if it takes less than two minutes.

29. You maximize Automobile University. You use every second in your commute time to boost your attitude and learn skills that will improve your personal and professional life.

30. You time block. You divide your day into time blocks of sixty to ninety minutes, with each time block having specific goals and objectives.

Skill Habits

31. You get clarity. Learning and using clarifying questions is one of the most powerful skills you can master.

32. You develop mentor–mentee relationships. A mentor who has already achieved success in an area you want to master is a huge help. Multiply this with being a good mentee—respect the mentor's time, ask good questions, take notes, implement his or her recommendations, report back on what you have implemented, repeat.

33. You listen. You practice active listening and confirm what is being said before taking action.

34. You communicate. You understand the personality style of the person you are talking to and speak in a way that is most effective for them.

35. You control your language. You avoid profanity. You use words that bring hope and encouragement and create the right environment for success.

36. You create routines. You develop routines in the day that maximize productivity and energy and allow you to own and control your attitude.

37. You choose to respond not react. You preplan how you are going to respond to challenges and setbacks rather than react to them based purely on emotion.

38. You have created a mission statement. You developed a personal mission statement that guides you in your career decisions regarding your character, integrity, and work ethic.

39. You have written-down goals. You clearly defined your goals and have written them down in detail with specific action plans.

40. You play the long game. You make decisions and develop your personal and professional skills based on your long-term objectives for your life.

41. You visualize how the right attitude, effort, and skill will change your life. Create a mental movie of yourself with a 10 out of 10 in attitude, effort, and skill, and imagine how your life will be different.

42. You reframe the negatives. When negative situations come up with other people, you take a moment to see their point of view and determine what would be a good outcome from their perspective.

43. You know your weaknesses and blind spots. You identify your blind spots and areas that are not natural strengths for you in your decision-making process and cultivate relationships that have these areas as their strengths.

44. You ask how and why. Instead of making your focus what you are going to do, you step back and ask yourself why and how you are going to do it as part of your process.

45. You mind map, which is a way to brainstorm. When beginning a major project or initiative, you create a mind map diagram that fosters new ideas around a single concept. This provides

a valuable overview of the project before you begin work on it.

46. You work on your soft skills. Your EQ, Emotional Quotient, is key to understanding the needs of other people, and until you understand the needs of those you are solving problems for, your performance will never be maximized.

47. You develop your *who*. Bob Beaudine, in *The Power of Who*, said, "You already know everyone you need to know to accomplish all that God has given you to do."[1] You develop and invest in your key friendships—they already know who you need to know.

48. You create your own personal development program. My dad said, "You have to be before you can do, and you have to do before you can have." You put together a plan to develop yourself so that you intentionally become a person who owns his or her attitude, effort, and skill.

49. You get regular feedback. You enlisted three or four people who want the best for you and who you can trust to give you constructive feedback in the areas of your attitude, effort, and skill.

50. You associate with those who have the same mind-set and beliefs. You identify the mind-set and beliefs that will help you achieve your goals and seek relationships with people who already have those beliefs and mind-sets.

You have what it takes. Time to get personal! Now go back and review all the items you marked as either a 1 or a 2. In each category—Attitude, Effort, and Skill—circle the three habits that if you moved to ownership level 3 would have the biggest impact on your success.

The fastest way to success is to replace bad habits with good habits. Get your pen out—it's time to take action!

THREE QUESTIONS TO TRANSFORMATION

I want you to write down the answers to these questions in your journal. Clarity helps you make the right choices and take the right actions!

1. What are my desires, dreams, and goals for my career or professional life? (Desire)
2. How will my life be better in the career or professional area when I work to solve the problems of others with the right attitude, effort, and skill? (Hope)
3. How can I apply grit to my gifts, talents, skills, and experience in the career or professional area of my life? (Grit)

Now it's time to develop the strategy and take action!

Step 1: Identify the Bad Career or Professional Habits You Have

What bad career or professional habits in the areas of attitude, effort (work ethic), and skill do you have that are keeping you from developing to your highest potential and keeping you from achieving your desires, dreams, and goals?

Write them down in your journal and be specific.

Step 2: Identify the Good Career or Professional Habits You Need

What input can you purposefully put into your mind, and what actions can you take, that will strengthen the career or professional qualities you want to develop that will allow you to achieve your desires, dreams, and goals faster (education, online courses, positive relationships like mentors or coaches, books, podcasts, self-talk, actions you can take, and so forth)?

Write them down in your journal and be specific.

Step 3: Choose to Replace a Bad Career or Professional Habit with a Good Career or Professional Habit

Pick a bad habit you want to replace with a good habit. Start small and build up. The key is starting and sticking with it! Each week you build on the same change from the previous week and/or replace another bad habit with a good habit.

Example: In the career or professional area of your life, you identify the bad habit of not being proactive regarding your attitude, effort, and skill. Your workday unfolds without a specific plan for creating a good attitude in yourself. Your effort is focused on putting out fires, and your professional skills are a result of on-the-job training, not strategic development based on where you want to be in five years. You determine that your lack of results and advancement is because you have not taken ownership of your attitude, effort, and skill. You decide that today is the day you take control of your most powerful economic engine—*you*. Today is the day you own your attitude, effort, and skill, and you are going to put in place the daily life-transforming choices in these three areas that change your career or professional future.

Bad career or professional habit: no proactive focus or ownership of my own attitude, effort, and skill.

Good career or professional habit: create a daily plan to raise my attitude, effort, and skill so that every week I am better than the previous, simply because of small good choices in each of these areas.

Here are four examples of how you can make small choices that will transform your life.

Example 1: Write a one-year goal detailing where I want to be in my career or professional life, and then identify the attitude I will need to achieve it, the effort I will need to reach my goal, and the skills I will need to develop in order to reach my goals. I will then break this one-year goal into ninety-day time periods and determine what I need to do in each area on a daily basis to hit my ninety-day time period goals. I will then track my progress in the area of attitude, effort, and skill each day and have a ninety-day review at the end of each time period and make adjustments as necessary.

Example 2: Determine and own that my career or professional attitude will be one of contagious positive encouragement and confidence that opens doors and builds trust. Each day I will start the day by taking ownership of my attitude and envisioning my attitude as the key to accomplishing my goals and solving the problems of others. Each day, and preferably at the start of the day, I will listen to, read, or have a purposeful, uplifting conversation with an accountability partner specifically in relationship to my attitude. This daily small choice of investing in my attitude five to fifteen minutes is key to my success.

Example 3: At the end of each day I will put together my work plan and to-do list for the next day and then review this first thing in the morning before my workday begins. My focus will be on priorities and the concept of working smoothly on the things that get the most results. This daily, ten-minute exercise keeps me laser-focused on my goals as I analyze each task in relationship to achieving my one-year goal.

Example 4: Each week I will set aside specific time for intentional skill development such as reading, online courses, attending a workshop, listening to a podcast, and so forth. On a daily basis I will use one idea, concept, or skill recently learned in my daily business activities and journal this or make a note in my Ziglar Performance Planner. Each day I will not go to bed until I have intentionally done one of these things at least once during the day. Do this for sixty-six days—the length of time it takes for this life-transforming small choice to become a habit.

Choose to win! Time to take action. Write down in your journal what you are going to intentionally do.

- List the bad career or professional habits you are going to get rid of.
- List the good career or professional habits you are going to implement.
- Write out the daily action plan to implement at least one good career or professional habit.

This may not seem like much, as it usually takes only a few minutes a day to implement a small good career or professional choice, but when you add to this every week, before you know it your life will be completely changed.

Can you feel it? Hope is rising over the tallest mountain because now you have a clear destination and specific choices and actions you can make that will get you there. Fuel your choices with grit, and developing your gifts and talents will fuel your balloon with rocket fuel!

WHEN DO I START?

One thing is certain: if you never take the first step, you will never take the second step.

In this final section of *Choose to Win*, I want to challenge you with several choices that will transform your life. Far too often people never start because they don't know where to start. Now that you know where to start, let's talk about *when* you start. Change begins with you, but it doesn't start until you do!

Your dream life is simply a series of choices done each day. As you start creating your dream life, consider these things:

You have to start to start.

You are going to leave a legacy, so make it intentional.

Starting is good; the perfect start—for you—is better.

Living a life of purpose, on purpose, is a choice.

Eternity is a long time!

Chapter 12
....

THE PERFECT START

W e're all going to leave a legacy. Will yours be by choice or by chance?

I believe you are destined for great things and God has hidden in your heart desires and passions that you are meant to pursue. The challenge is that the world and everyday life bury these desires and passions under mounds of obligations, doubts, and fears. We get so caught up in the struggle of day-to-day life that we forget our purpose, what we are made for, and instead settle for what the world says we should do. Even worse, we begin to believe the lie that we are not good enough and don't deserve to pursue our desires and dreams. Now is the time. Today is the day you choose to pursue your desires and dreams and leave a legacy by design, not by chance!

THREE CHOICES

I am going to challenge you right now to make three choices that will change your life and your legacy. These three choices move your dreams out of your imagination and into reality. These three choices make the impossible possible and the overwhelming as simple as taking one step. These three choices turn your "I wish" into "I will" and your "I will" into "I did."

Choice 1: Go Ahead and Take the First Step

Something big is on your heart, something "God"-sized that you know you are meant to do.

Just start.

I don't know how.
I have never done that before.
What if I look like a fool?

Just start.

Other people do this sort of thing, not me.
I barely know anything about it.
It's hard.

Just start.

I will be fifty-five years old next month.
There is a lot of competition out there.
Nobody in my family has ever done that.

Just start.

Take the first step.
Write it down as a goal.
Invest twenty minutes a day learning about it.

Something big is on your heart.

If you could do it alone, with what you have, it wouldn't be big enough, would it?

Choice 2: Choose to Leave a Legacy by Design

In my travels around the world I have made an interesting observation. I will ask the audience I am speaking to this question: "Raise your hand if you want to leave a legacy that will ripple through eternity." Every time I ask this question, 100 percent of the hands go up!

I am sure you want to leave a legacy that will ripple through eternity too. Following are five steps you can take to build your legacy by design.

1. Be intentional.

    Are you going to leave a legacy by design or by chance? Either way, one thing is certain: you are going to leave a legacy! Be intentional by first determining what you want your legacy to be. What words, principles, and values do you want your family to be known for? What do you want your family brand and reputation to be? When people talk about your family, what do they say? Now claim the words and phrases that you want your family to be known for. The Ziglar family is known for *hope* and *encouragement, character* and *integrity,* and *persistent consistency.* Words like *love, grateful, kind, courage, servant's heart,* and *followers of Christ* are all good words for the legacy you are creating by design. Once you have the words and phrases for your family, it's time to take action. And remember, it's never too late to start. You can start making small choices today that will impact your legacy, no matter what stage of life you are in.

2. Create daily legacy moments.

    Do you have sixty seconds a day to intentionally create a legacy that will ripple through eternity? Do you know how to send a text, leave a voice mail, write a short note, have a short conversation? Of course you do! A daily legacy moment is simply intentionally using one of your family words in a way that builds your family's legacy. For example, one of your kids demonstrates your family's word of *courage* by sticking up for a classmate who is being bullied at school. Write your child a note or send a text that says, "I am so proud of you and how you had the courage to stand by your friend yesterday when she was being made fun of by the other kids. Keep it up!"

This simple, small choice has a massive impact. Tyson Murphy, one of my clients with whom I have had the privilege of working in my executive coaching program, implemented this concept with his family. Every day before school or before he heads off to the office, Tyson writes each of his children a short note telling them how much he cares for them and letting them know he is thinking of them. Just three weeks after he started this, Tyson's wife, Lacey, joined us for a coaching session in our offices. Lacey and Tyson both were overwhelmed with emotion as they shared the impact the little notes were having. "At first the kids didn't know what to think, but now they kinda wait around for their note," Tyson said. The expression on Lacey's face said it all to me. This simple, small choice was connecting their family in ways they had never imagined.

3. Plan weekly legacy dinners.

Do you and your family eat on a regular basis? Of course you do! The challenge is weekly family dinners are often rushed and filled with distractions, if they happen at all. It's time to take back your family! Once a week, plan to have a ten-minute family discussion around something that is happening in your life in relationship to your family words.

A weekly legacy dinner is simply starting a discussion at mealtime with your family about a current event or life happening and then using your family words to determine how your family responds to the situation. For example, use a hot media topic or a situation at school that everyone is talking about. As a family, discuss what the world or the school is doing about it and what the family can do about it. Use your family words in the discussion, like, "How can we talk to others about this situation using our family words of *love, kindness,* and *integrity*?"

4. Plan a monthly legacy event.

This is similar to a legacy dinner, but it is much more intentional as your purpose is to plan a two-hour event where your legacy words come to life. A legacy event doesn't have to be complicated, it just needs to break the routine. You could pack a picnic lunch and take a board game with you to a local park. This will create a good memory, and when you talk about life and your family words, the message will become real. Another idea would be taking a lunch as a family to a neighbor who is a widow or who is unable to easily get out of the house. Demonstrating a family word is much more powerful than talking about it!

5. Plan a yearly legacy experience.

Once a year do something big around your family words. You can make a legacy experience incredible with just a little bit of preplanning, and this will give you many opportunities throughout the year to have intentional conversations about your family. A couple of simple ideas you can use: If you are planning a family vacation, do something that creates a memory. Build a huge sandcastle with your family words made in sand and take a family picture. Visit a historical site or museum, and as your family learns things, ask each member to find one example of each family word during the day. If you have a family reunion or extended family get-togethers around holidays, get your extended family members to tell the old stories and legends of the family. You could ask an uncle, "What was the greatest act of *kindness* that you saw Grandpa do?"

You are building your legacy right now. The only question is, will your legacy be by design or by chance? These five steps will help you build your legacy by design.

Choice 3: Choose to Start Each Day with the Perfect Start

....

"The difference between who you are and
who you want to be, is what you do."

—BILL PHILLIPS

....

The most powerful habit in my life is what I call the Perfect Start. I believe when you choose this habit every area of your life will improve.

The Perfect Start is simply how you start each day. The goal is simple: to make your life happen to your day rather than the day happen to your life. Each day I intentionally invest the first part of the day to build myself, plan the day, and accomplish my top priorities. Before I lay out my personal Perfect Start, I want to share with you a few things to keep in mind.

It doesn't matter if you are a morning person. If you're not, that is okay. Your Perfect Start can be tailored to your needs and it can be short. The key is to get your mind working and thinking intentionally on what you need to accomplish before you head off to work.

Start small. I invest ninety minutes or longer in my Perfect Start, but I didn't start that way. Ten minutes, even five minutes, as you learn this new habit is fine. The key is doing it every day until it becomes a habit. I would rather you do ten minutes a day every day for sixty-six days than to do thirty minutes three or four times a week. The Perfect Start is a muscle you build. Don't run a marathon your first time out!

Remove distractions. I do my Perfect Start first thing every morning. I get up, make the coffee, and begin. I don't check email, text messages, social media, the news, and so on, until after my Perfect Start. The goal is to get your mind-set right first, then plan the day, then tackle objectives for the day.

Create the time. Do the Perfect Start first thing. Create the time by getting up a little bit earlier, if need be. It is amazing how getting up fifteen minutes earlier and using those fifteen minutes in the Perfect Start pays you back all day long.

Here is my Perfect Start, with explanations and ideas you can use. Don't limit yourself to only what I suggest—make the Perfect Start *your* Perfect Start.

I do my Perfect Start in my study where it is quiet and distraction-free.

Time	Activity
5 minutes	This is my prayer and quiet time with God. I learned this technique from Bob Beaudine, who wrote the book *2 Chairs*. I describe it in chapter 3. This is an amazing way to start the day. Other things you can do in this time are meditation and reflection on things you are grateful for.
20 minutes	Reading Scripture and devotionals. The number one lesson Dad taught me was to choose the right input for my life. I start with God's Word. This builds me up both mentally and spiritually. You can also read inspirational and educational books that are uplifting and help develop you into the person you want to become. Ziglar Self-Talk affirmation cards are excellent to read out loud to yourself during this time.

5 minutes	Journaling. I write a brief entry every day—one to five sentences on my thinking, feeling, and insights. What a great way to remember what's important.
10 minutes	The Ziglar Performance Planner. I write out my daily goals, objectives, and to-dos for the day and review the previous day to see if I did what I said I was going to do. I love the intentionality of this because it gives me a plan and a lot of peace about what I intend to accomplish during the day. This keeps me accountable and moving forward on my major goals. We covered the goal-setting system in chapter 3, and this is where I track my progress each day.
5 minutes	The mental model. In my Performance Planner I write down the important phone calls, face-to-face meetings, and presentations I have scheduled for the day. I then do a sixty-second "mental model" of how I envision each one of these appointments going. I anticipate what questions and needs the other people may have. I think about their personality styles and what outcomes would be win-win-win. It is amazing how spending just sixty seconds on each appointment for the day impacts the outcomes so positively.
45 minutes	The One Thing. What is the most important objective you need to accomplish? It could be finishing a project, writing your book, cleaning out your inbox, working out, and so forth. The key here is to do something that is important and not necessarily urgent. As you can imagine, for me this is normally either writing or preparing for a presentation. The good news is, you get to decide your one thing.

There you have it, my Perfect Start. What will yours look like? It's up to you!

If you don't know where to start or you don't have much time, I suggest you start this way.

3 minutes	Write down three things you are grateful for and meditate on the good things going on in your life.
3 minutes	Read one of the Ziglar Self-Talk Cards or something equally as uplifting and inspirational.
4 minutes	Write down your major goals and to-dos for the day and keep the list with you to keep you on track.

Your turn! Create your own Perfect Start.

Review your big *why*, your desires, your dreams, and your goals. Reflect on the legacy you want to leave, and imagine the power and impact *Just Start* will have on your life. Now create your own Perfect Start that will help make these a reality in your own life. Create the Perfect Start in your journal under the headings "Time" and "Activity," using mine as a model.

Chapter 13
....

CHOOSE TO LIVE A
LIFE OF PURPOSE

Living a life of purpose is a choice. I believe we are all created on purpose and for a purpose. I also know that almost everyone struggles with this at some point in their life. After all, how do you know if you are living out your purpose?

Following are three choices you can make that will guide you as you live out your life of purpose. The inspiration for these three choices came from Fred Smith Jr., the son of Fred Smith, who was Dad's mentor.

1. CHOOSE TO KNOW THE SOURCE
OF YOUR GIFTS AND TALENTS

I love this simple concept. Choose to *know* the Source. I believe your Creator wants to have a relationship with you. This is not about religion, it's about relationship. This is why Bob Beaudine's *2 Chairs* concept is so powerful. Imagine God showing up to have a conversation with you, one-on-one. He will!

Now that you are seeking a relationship with the Source of your gifts and talents, something magical happens. You are forced to realize you are special, unique, and no one in the universe is like you. Recognizing God as the Source of your gifts and talents creates an attitude of gratitude in your spirit. Thanking God for what He has given you unleashes the power trapped inside of you. You have gifts and talents only you can use, and God has people waiting for you to use your gifts and talents so He can bless them through you!

My friend Trenell Walker lives an incredible life of purpose. Trenell's life has not been easy. When he was fourteen, he was paralyzed from the neck down in a football accident. In an instant everything changed for him. Over time, and still to this day, Trenell is growing in his relationship with God, and his unique gifts and talents are being honed as iron sharpens iron. Trenell is a powerful speaker and coach, and when he speaks, you listen. God's power, combined with Trenell's unique gifts and talents, are changing many lives, including mine. Trenell reaches people few of us can reach because his adversity and how he has chosen to handle it are a testimony no one can dismiss.

"But wait," you say. "How can this be? Terrible things have happened to me, and I have done terrible things." God knows. And He is waiting for you to ask Him these questions. He has an answer for you only your soul can hear. Seek to know Him, and He will answer the questions of your heart.

2. CHOOSE TO WORK ON YOUR GIFTS AND TALENTS WITH GRIT

In chapter 4, "Desire, Hope, and Grit," grit is the knob on the furnace of your hot air balloon. Grit is the difference maker, the maximizer, the unstoppable force. However, grit only gets maximum results when it is applied to your unique gifts and talents. What are your gifts and talents? Throughout this book we have given you tools and ideas to help you identify your gifts and talents, along with dozens of habits you can build that will allow your gifts and talents to grow. The parable of the talents is found in Matthew 25. Your purpose is found not in what the master didn't give you, but in what the master did give you.

My dad was raised in poverty, never did well in school, didn't graduate from college, had a very tough start in sales, and had small dreams when he was a young man. Yet God gave him an incredible voice and the ability to communicate the complex in very simple terms. Most people don't realize that Dad invested three hours a day for more than forty years reading, researching, and perfecting how he would communicate life's most important lessons. Zig Ziglar's legacy lives on today because he was grateful for the gifts God gave him and worked on them with grit for the majority of his life.

3. CHOOSE TO SHARE YOUR GIFTS AND TALENTS WITH HUMILITY AND LOVE

Boom! There it is! When you share your gifts and talents with humility and love, they are received and the impact is exponential—for you and the receiver—just as God intended it. Ego, motive, selfishness—each of these diminish our gifts and talents. The world is changed, one life at a time, when we simply follow the process of knowing the Source and being grateful for our gifts and talents, working on them with grit, and sharing them with humility and love.

When Dad was eighty years old, he had a terrible fall down the stairs that resulted in a TBI, a traumatic brain injury. This took away his short-term memory and changed the way he was able to give speeches. The last four years of Dad's speaking career were done in an interview format with my sister Julie. Julie would let the crowd know why she was there, explain Dad's injury, and then ask Dad questions and he would answer. If Dad repeated himself, Julie would remind him he had already said that and get him back on track. We got overwhelmingly positive feedback from these presentations, but we were still concerned how Dad was coming across, as we wanted the best for Dad.

When Dad was speaking in Green Bay, Wisconsin, one of Julie's psychologist friends was in the audience. Julie asked her friend to listen to the interview she did with Dad, watch the crowd's response, and let her know if Dad was being well received. At the end of the day, Julie's friend told her there was nothing to be concerned about. She told Julie that she had heard a lot of great speakers that day (there were nine top speakers, experts, and celebrities), but only one of the speakers was there just for the audience. Dad's love and concern for the audience of ten thousand plus was still palpable. Yes, when you share your gifts and talents with love, it changes everything and allows you to fulfill God's purpose for you, no matter your "limitations."

I BELIEVE!

How can I not believe?

I believe you can live a *Choose to Win* life, a life lived on purpose for a purpose. In fact, I believe we are all called for an eternal purpose. Many people from different faith backgrounds have asked me a simple question: "Why do you believe in Christ?" My answer is always the same: "How can I not believe?" And then I share with them Dad's last few days on earth and a few of the miracles I witnessed.

It was Thanksgiving Day 2012, and it was going to be the first Thanksgiving that our family would not have our traditional family meal together because of Dad's failing health. Our plan was to visit Dad, who was receiving full-time health care, and then eat as a family after our time with him. Dad's Alzheimer's was becoming severe at this stage of his life.

When we walked into his room, we knew immediately that something major was wrong. Dad was having trouble breathing as they worked on him, and minutes later we were rushing to the hospital. They admitted Dad and started doing everything they could for him. A little while later they called us into the private waiting room where nobody wants to go.

The doctor told us, "Your father's condition is very serious. We have done everything we can, and we will know in about forty-five minutes if he is going to make it."

Gut punch. Shock. I bet you have had similar news in your life and you can understand how we were all feeling.

Before I knew it, we were back in the waiting room with the doctor. "Your father is not responding. He doesn't have much time left. Go now and be with him."

Stunned, I sat there with my wife and daughter as the rest of the family went to be with Dad. After everyone but the three of us had left the room, I looked up to see the doctor holding the door open. "You're the son, aren't you?" he said. "I have seen this before. Go *now* and be with your father." In a daze, I went down to be with Dad.

As we spent time with Dad, he started to rally, and the decision was made to move him into a room where we would have more privacy. They told us he would likely pass away in the next few hours. Dad was now comfortable but noncommunicative.

The hours stretched late into the night when my sister Julie said she needed to show us something. She pulled out her iPhone and showed us a five-second video she had made a few weeks earlier driving home from visiting Mom and Dad. On the video was a beautiful cloud in the shape of a Z. It was perfect, as if a heavenly artist had put it there on purpose. None of us had ever seen a cloud in the shape of a Z before. We knew that very soon we were going to have to share the news of Dad's passing, and we decided to make a banner for our website and Facebook featuring the Z cloud. *What a beautiful way to remember Dad*, we thought.

The next morning I texted a few of our close friends. Pastors Jill and Jay Hellwig, who both worked with us for years, came right away. They immediately began to pray over Dad, and you could feel the peace in the room. After a little while, Jill backed out of the room into the hallway. I was watching her as she left, and I saw her look up above the doorway. A big smile broke out on her face, and she began to laugh joyously.

"What are you laughing at?" I asked her.

"This is perfect!" she said. "The number over the doorway represents 'new beginning' in Hebrew."

Four hours later I realized how perfect that number was.

A New Beginning

A few hours after Jill and Jay left, I got a call from my good friend Billy Cox. Billy was close to Dad and viewed Dad as a mentor and friend who had greatly helped him during his life. As I spoke to Billy, I could tell he was distraught, and I encouraged him to come right over. When Billy arrived, I could see the grief, concern, and worry on his face. He immediately grabbed Dad's hand and began to pray silently. I saw Billy's face relax as peace spread over his countenance.

After a few minutes, Billy turned to me and said, "Tom, I am so sorry I didn't get your text right away. I was taking a nap—which I never do. I thought I had missed being able to say good-bye to your dad. I was taking a nap because a few nights ago I didn't get much sleep and I needed to catch up. I didn't sleep well that night because I was dreaming about your dad. Tom, I have never had a dream about your dad before. Have you ever had a dream that is so powerful it wakes you and then when you fall back asleep the dream starts again? This happened to me six or seven times. In my dream I was sitting at a table with your dad and I was looking at him and kept saying, 'Zig, is it over? *Is it over?*' And every time I asked your dad that, he looked me in the eye and said, 'No, Billy, it's a new beginning.'"

We were blessed with almost a week of time with Dad before he finally took his last breath. The next day we met with Jack Graham, Dad's pastor, who would be doing the funeral. Pastor Graham pulled out Dad's file, and in it was a letter written by Dad that contained a detailed outline of the funeral service. All we had to do was pick who was going to sing the songs and decide if we wanted someone to deliver a message. Dad had made it clear that his funeral was going to be a celebration and that the hope found in Jesus would be shared.

As we were leaving, I realized we had discussed the main service at the church but not the graveside service. The graveside service was scheduled for family and close friends at 9:00 a.m., and the church service would be held at 11:00 a.m.

"Pastor," I said, "how should we do the graveside?"

"How would you like it?" he responded.

"Short and sweet, since everything is covered in the main service," I answered.

"Perfect, I agree, and I will take care of everything," Pastor Graham replied.

Later that day I called Julie on the phone to see how she was doing.

"So happy for Dad, so sad for me," she said. I can still hear her saying that. That is exactly how we all felt.

The next afternoon we were all with Mom at her place, getting ready to go to the visitation at the funeral home. "Hey, y'all, I have something to show you," Julie said and pulled up the Z-cloud video. "I just remembered the video has audio on it. Let's listen to the message."

She replayed the video with the sound turned all the way up. The person on the radio in the five-second clip mentioned a Bible passage: 1 Thessalonians 4:13–18. We looked at each other and grabbed one of Dad's Bibles to see what the passage said.

Here it is:

> But we do not want you to be uninformed, brothers, about those who
> are asleep, that you may not grieve as others do who have no hope.
> For since we believe that Jesus died and rose again, even so, through
> Jesus, God will bring with him those who have fallen asleep. For this
> we declare to you by a word from the Lord, that we who are alive, who
> are left until the coming of the Lord, will not precede those who have
> fallen asleep. For the Lord himself will descend from heaven with a
> cry of command, with the voice of an archangel, and with the sound
> of the trumpet of God. And the dead in Christ will rise first. Then we
> who are alive, who are left, will be caught up together with them in
> the clouds to meet the Lord in the air, and so we will always be with
> the Lord. Therefore encourage one another with these words.

We couldn't believe it! God had given us the perfect message for exactly the right time. We went to the visitation filled with hope and encouragement, even though we were grieving.

First Thessalonians 4:13–18 spoke to our time of need. Verse 13 says to "not grieve as others do who have no hope." Our hope is Jesus, and in Him is eternal life. Plus, the word *hope* has huge meaning for us Ziglars. *60 Minutes* named Dad "the Merchant of Hope," and Dad believed his primary message was to bring hope and encouragement to the world. Verse 14 was the perfect message, reminding us that Christ died and rose again so that we all could have eternal life. For good measure, verse 17 has the word *clouds* in it, a clear reminder to us that the Z cloud was put there by God for Julie to see. And this passage ends with verse 18, "Therefore encourage one another"—Dad's greatest gift, the gift of encouragement. In fact, as I have mentioned, the Sunday school class that Dad taught for many years was called the Encouragers Class.

The next morning we were all seated for the graveside service. Pastor Graham walked out to start the service and said, "Let me share a Bible passage with you: 1 Thessalonians 4:13–18." My sisters and I made eye contact—we couldn't believe it! The same passage! When the service was over, I went to Pastor Graham. "Did someone by chance show you the Z-cloud video?" I asked. He had no clue what I was talking about. We all left and made our way to the church for the big service. It was beautiful, and Dad's wishes were fulfilled.

(You can watch the Z-cloud video right here. Turn up the sound!)

ziglar.com/zcloud

HOW CAN I NOT BELIEVE?

I believe you and I were created for a purpose, that we are born to win, and we can live to win!

I believe, like Dad, that all of us are designed for accomplishment, engineered for success, and endowed with the seeds of greatness. I believe that Christ came that we might have life and have it more abundantly and that Christ died that we might live.

I pray you are richly blessed and that God reveals Himself to you in a mighty way. I encourage you to spend a few minutes alone with Him, simply asking Him the questions on your heart. Listen carefully—I believe He has a word just for you.

Go ahead . . . *choose to win!* A life of purpose awaits you. Success, significance, and legacy are the results of good small choices done over and over again, and you have what it takes! Transforming into the person God created you to be is within your grasp. Start now from where you are with what you have and add just a little bit extra every single day, one small choice at a time. If you do, your legacy will ripple through eternity.

Choose to win!

ADDENDUM

Now for the *How*

The Ziglar Goals Setting System is tried and true. For more than four decades, hundreds of thousands of people have used this system to get what they want. I encourage you to read this next section several times. The first time to get an overview. The second time to start thinking more deeply about your dreams that you want to turn into goals and then into reality. The third time to go through it as an active participant, investing the time necessary to get your dreams and goals out of your head and onto paper.

Why? Dad said it best:

....

"A goal properly set is halfway reached."

....

THE ZIGLAR GOALS SETTING SYSTEM

Action Step 1

Create your dream list. Let your imagination run wild and write down everything you want to be, do, or have. If you have a family, be sure to include your mate and children when you set your goals. This entire goals-setting process helps channel your logical left brain and your creative right brain for more effective use of your imagination.

Your dream list is best created over a two- to three-day time frame. Start by writing every dream you have and goal you want to achieve: the person you want to become, the things you want to do (career, activities, and so on), and things you want to have (your dream house, savings account, and so on). Your initial list may have fifteen, twenty, even fifty things on it. Now, during the next seventy-two hours, add to it. Plan some time in the morning or evening to revisit the list and add to it. Many people plan a dream weekend to create their list. Record your goals and dreams in your journal under the heading: Things I Really Want to Be, Do, and Have List.

Tip: My good friends Karen and Paul Sullivan plan annual dream weekends when they go to a peaceful place to review their dreams and goals. Each of them has an active list of a hundred goals and dreams they would like to achieve. Each year they start by marking off the goals and dreams they achieved the previous year. They then each add new dreams and goals and eliminate goals that are no longer important. Here is the cool part: they trade lists so that they know each other's dreams and goals, and throughout the year they actively seek to find ways to help each other achieve their goals. For example, if Paul knows Karen wants to travel to a certain city, he will let her know when he has a business trip near that location and they plan the trip together. How awesome is it when those you love are helping you achieve your goals?

Action Step 2

Wait twenty-four to forty-eight hours and then answer the question *why* for each item you have written on your dream list. Use a different color pen and in one sentence verbalize why you want to be, do, or have what you have written down. If you can't answer the question why, then it isn't a real goal or dream, so go ahead and cross it off your list.

Action Step 3

Ask these five questions for each dream or goal on your list. All five questions must be answered with a yes for the dream or goal to stay on your list.

1. *Is it really my goal?* If you're a minor living at home, an employee, or a team member, some of your goals will be set by your coach, director, parent, or employer.
2. *Is it morally right and fair to everyone concerned?* Some goals may take so much time or attention that they hurt relationships with others. A goal to walk across the United States might be a great goal when you're single and twenty-two but not if you're married and have three kids under the age of five.
3. *Is it consistent with my other goals?* You can't have a goal to win the Nathan's hotdog eating contest and be in perfect physical health at the same time.
4. *Can I emotionally commit myself to finish this goal?* Are you all in?
5. *Can I see myself reaching this goal?*

Note: Answering these questions will further reduce the number of dreams on your Things I Really Want to Be, Do, or Have list, so scratch any nos off the list. Answering questions 2 and 3 will be very helpful in making important decisions in all areas of life, especially financial.

Action Step 4

After each remaining dream ask yourself these questions:
Will reaching this goal make me . . .

happier?
healthier?
more prosperous?
have more friends?
have more peace of mind?
more secure?
improve my relationships with others?
have hope in the future?

If you can't answer yes to at least one of these questions, eliminate that item from your list of dreams. Careful: Don't confuse pleasure with happiness. Be sure to consider your family when you answer these questions.

Action Step 5

Divide the remaining goals into three categories:

- Short-range (one month or less)
- Intermediate (one month to one year)
- Long-range (one year or more)

Now mark them SR (short-range), I (intermediate), or LR (long-range) on your Things I Really Want to Be, Do, or Have list. *Go ahead. Do it now.* By taking this step you will be able to quickly determine whether or not you have a balanced perspective between what needs to be done now versus your dreams for the future.

Remember:

- *Some* goals must be big (out of reach, not out of sight) to make you stretch and grow to your full potential.
- *Some* goals must be long-range to keep you on track and greatly reduce the possibility of short-range frustrations.
- *Some* goals must be small and daily to keep you disciplined and in touch with the reality of the "nitty-gritties" of daily life.
- *Some* goals must be ongoing.
- *Some* goals (sales, educational, financial, weight loss, and so on) might require analysis and consultation to determine where you are before you can set the goals.
- *Most* goals should be specific. A "nice home" is not as good as "three-thousand-square-foot, Tudor-style home with four bedrooms, three full baths, two living spaces." Some goals, like improving your self-image, becoming a better parent, or getting a better education, are more difficult to pinpoint. Those that are less specific should be broken down into specific, tangible steps. For instance, a step to becoming a better parent could be "spend one hour per week one-on-one with each child."

Action Step 6

From the remaining goals, prayerfully choose the four goals (remember balance is the key) that are most important to you right now. Write down those goals in your journal.

If this is your first organized goal-setting experience, you may want to start with two or three short-range goals.

Important: Now create a Charting My Progress page in your journal and record these goals (Goal/Date Started/Date Reached). You will be encouraged tremendously as you record the goals you reach throughout the year, so make sure to add the new goals you are working on to this page. Your confidence, self-image, and goals-achieving ability will improve dramatically.

Action Step 7

Record these four goals on a Goals Procedure Chart you create in your journal (instructions follow) or go to www.ziglar.com/ChooseToWin to download copies. You may also want to consider the Ziglar Performance Planner, which is the one-year Ziglar goals-tracking journal you can use to work on your goals every day, which is also found at www.ziglar.com /ChooseToWin.

GENERAL GOALS PROCEDURE CHART

Following is an example of a goal I set while writing this book. This example will help you better understand how to fill out a General Goals Procedure Chart for your own goals. (See page 8 of the Ziglar Performance Planner.)

Step 1: Identify Your Goal

I enjoy weighing a healthy 185 pounds with a 36-inch waist.

Tip: Make your goal first-person, present tense. Your subconscious mind will work to make this a reality as you focus on it every day.

Step 2: My Benefits to Reaching This Goal

- More energy, less illness
- Look and feel better
- More confidence
- Longer life span
- Better endurance
- More productivity

- Better concentration and clarity
- Better attitude and disposition
- More creativity
- Better example
- Lower health care and insurance costs
- Able to chase the grandkids I hope to have

Tip: The longer and more detailed the list of benefits, the more likely you are to stick with it. Fill up this section and get others to give you ideas on additional benefits.

Step 3: Major Obstacles and Mountains to Climb to Reach This Goal

- Lack of discipline
- Travel schedule
- Love of carbs
- Bad eating habits, such as eating late at night
- Poor physical condition
- Time

Step 4: Skills and Knowledge Required to Reach This Goal

- Healthy eating knowledge based on my body type
- Exercise routines I can use based on my physical condition
- How to get better sleep

Step 5: Individuals, Groups, Companies, and Organizations to Work with to Reach This Goal

- Dr. Randall James
- Nutritionist
- Chachis
- Scott Eriksson—NERDbody

Step 6: Plan of Action to Reach This Goal

- Make commitment to track daily
- Fasting between 7:30 p.m. and 11:00 a.m.
- 4 x daily NERDbody or movement
- 4 x weekly walking thirty-plus minutes each
- Low-carb diet and stay away from processed foods and chemicals
- Drink 100 ounces of water per day
- Always have a healthy snack with me

Step 7: Completion Date

Now it's your turn! Set a realistic date for completion of this goal. Go ahead, write your own goal in your journal, using the following headings, or download the worksheet from www.ziglar.com/ChooseToWin.

Step 1: Identify Your Goal

Step 2: My Benefits to Reaching This Goal

Step 3: Major Obstacles and Mountains to Climb to Reach This Goal

Step 4: Skills and Knowledge Required to Reach This Goal

Step 5: Individuals, Groups, Companies, and Organizations to Work with to Reach This Goal

Step 6: Plan of Action to Reach This Goal

Step 7: Completion Date

Step 8: Complete General Goals Procedure Chart

Take the additional goals you have listed on your Things I Really Want to Be, Do, or Have list and record each on a General Goals Procedure Chart. Work each goal through the process as you did in Action Steps 1–7. Remember, you can download this entire activity with sample worksheets or purchase the Ziglar Performance Planner at www.ziglar.com/ChooseToWin.

Do it now. Remember, motivation comes after you start the project.

———

Congratulations! You have invested more time in planning your future than most of your friends, relatives, and associates will ever invest. Now comes the fun part. You have turned your dreams into goals, now it's time to turn your goals into reality!

It is time to start investing eight minutes a day reviewing and working on your goals. Again, I recommend the Ziglar Performance Planner for this, but I want to give you a simple process and a work-sheet you can use to start right now.

Begin by writing down the four goals you are going to work on for the week. Then each day write down what you are going to do that day to work on that goal. The next day write down what you actually accomplished the previous day on that goal, and write down what you are going to do that day. Repeat daily. A great practice is to review your goals first thing in the morning before the day starts and last thing at night before you go to sleep. Nothing is better than dreaming about achieving your dreams and goals.

One of my dad's habits was to work on his goals in the morning and then put the Performance Planner under his pillow on the bed. This way, when he got in bed for the night, he would review his goals again. This is truly eight minutes that will change your life!

Create a Weekly Personal Performance Record in your journal (or you can download at www.ziglar.com/ChooseToWin).

TO-DOS

Now you know how to get what you want! The hard part is done, the rest is just work.

I have a challenge for you. Think about the top four goals you would like to achieve in the next twelve months. How much would it be worth to you if you achieved even just a couple of them? Depending on the goal you set, it could be worth thousands of dollars, or incredible personal satisfaction, or better relationships at home and at work. If you were to achieve a health or fitness goal, what price can you put on that? The question, my friend, is not, "Is it worth it?" The question to ask yourself is, "Will I do what I need to do when I need to do it so that the day will come when I can do what I want to do when I want to do it?"

A simple thought for you: People tend to overestimate what they can achieve in a short period of time, and they underestimate what they can achieve over a long period of time. *Choose to Win* is about the long game. It's about making the right choices and doing the right small things on a daily basis that, over time, will create an amazing life. You are on the right path, and you have what it takes!

If you are not sure how or where to start, why not start with First Things First?

Many times people get overwhelmed with goal setting and how or where to start on their own plan. Now that you know how to set a good goal, let me give you a place to start so you can start building the habit of creating good habits.

For the first month of your goal-setting and achieving journey, and maybe forever, I recommend that one of your goals is to review your goals and record your priorities before you do any other work—including checking email, texts, or social media. I call this the Perfect Start. This is what I do every day, and doing First Things First is one of my permanent, ongoing goals (p. 44).

ZIGLAR SELF-TALK CARDS

A Life-Changing Procedure

*T**he eyes are the windows of the soul. So, to the person you are capable of becoming, each evening, just before you go to bed, stand in front of a mirror alone and in the first-person, present tense, look yourself in the eye and repeat with passion and enthusiasm paragraphs A, B, C, and D. Repeat this process every morning and every evening from this day forward. Within one week you will notice remarkable changes in your life. After thirty days add the procedure at the bottom of this card.*

A

"I, _____, am an honest, intelligent, organized, responsible, committed, teachable person who is sober, loyal, and clearly understands that regardless of who signs my paycheck I am self-employed. I am an optimistic, punctual, enthusiastic, goal-setting, smart working self-starter who is a disciplined, focused, dependable, persistent positive thinker with great self-control, and am an energetic and diligent team player and hard worker who appreciates the opportunity my company and the free enterprise system offer me. I am thrifty with my resources and apply common sense to my daily tasks. I take honest pride in my competence, appearance and manners, and am motivated to be and do my best so that my healthy self-image will remain on solid ground. These are the qualities that enable me to manage myself and help give me employment security in a no-job-security world.

B

"I, _____, am a compassionate, respectful encourager who is a considerate, generous, gentle, patient, caring, sensitive, personable, attentive, fun-loving person. I am a supportive, giving and forgiving, clean, kind, unselfish, affectionate, loving, family-oriented human being and I am a sincere and open-minded good listener and a good-finder who is trustworthy. These are the qualities that enable me to build good relationships with my associates, neighbors, mate, and family.

C

"I, _____, am a person of integrity, with the faith and wisdom to know what I should do and the courage and convictions to follow through. I have the vision to manage myself and to lead others. I am authoritative, confident, and humbly grateful for the opportunity life offers me. I am fair, flexible, resourceful, creative, knowledgeable, decisive, and an extra-miler with a servant's attitude who communicates well with others. I am a consistent, pragmatic teacher with character and a finely tuned sense of humor. I am an honorable person and am balanced in my personal, family, and business life, and have a passion for being, doing, and learning more today so I can be, do, and have more tomorrow.

D

"These are the qualities of the winner I was born to be, and I am fully committed to developing these marvelous qualities with which I have been entrusted. Tonight I'm going to sleep wonderfully well. I will dream powerful, positive dreams. I will awaken energized and refreshed; tomorrow's going to be magnificent, and my future is unlimited. Recognizing, claiming, and developing these qualities that I already have gives me a legitimate chance to be happier, healthier, more prosperous, more secure, have more friends, greater peace of mind, better family relationships, and legitimate hope that the future will be even better."

REPEAT THE PROCESS THE NEXT MORNING AND CLOSE BY SAYING:

"These are the qualities of the winner I was born to be, and I will develop and use these qualities to achieve my worthy objectives. Today is a brand-new day, and it's mine to use in a marvelously productive way."

AFTER 30 DAYS, ADD THE NEXT STEP:

Choose your strongest quality and the one you feel needs the most work. Example: Strongest—honest. Needs most work—organized. On a separate 3 x 5 card, print "I, _____, am a completely honest person, and every day I am getting better and better organized." Keep this 3 x 5 card handy and read it out loud at every opportunity for one week. Repeat this process with the second-strongest quality and the second one that needs the most work. Do this until you've completed the entire list. Use this self-talk procedure as long as you want to get more of the things money will buy and all the things money won't buy.

Note: Because of some painful experiences in the past (betrayal, abuse, etc.), there might be a word or two that brings back unpleasant memories (example: *discipline*). Eliminate the word or substitute another word.

MY PERSONAL COMMITMENT

I, _____, am serious about setting and reaching my goals in my life, so on this _____day of _____, 20_____, I promise myself that I will take the first step toward setting those goals.

I am willing to exchange temporary pleasures in the pursuit of happiness and the striving for excellence in the pursuit of my goals. I am willing to discipline my physical and emotional appetites to reach the long-range goals of happiness and accomplishment. I recognize that to reach my goals I must grow personally and have the right mental attitude, so I promise to specifically increase my knowledge in my chosen field and regularly read positive-growth books and magazines. I will also attend lectures and seminars, take courses in personal growth and development. I will use my time more effectively by enrolling in Automobile University and listening to motivational and educational recordings, while driving or performing routine tasks at home or in the yard. I will keep a list of my activities, including the completion dates for each project, in my Goals Program. I further promise to list good ideas (mine and those of others) and to note thoughts, power-phrases, and quotations that have meaning to me.

Date   Signature

ACKNOWLEDGMENTS

To my beautiful wife, Chachis, and my amazing daughter, Alexandra, who motivate and inspire me every day. My sisters, Cindy and Julie, who encourage me in everything I do. To my agent, close friend, and confidant for more than twenty years, Bruce Barbour. My *Who* friend, Bob Beaudine, whom I leave the planet with as we dream about all that God has in store for us.

My friend, business partner, biggest supporter, and the man who has helped me grow more than anyone outside of my dad, Howard Partridge. Michael Norton, my "rope man" and friend, who loves changing lives almost as much as I do. Scott Eriksson, my close friend and "little brother," who gets me to think differently on just about everything. David Wright, my coaching partner, who draws out the best in everyone, including me. Laurie Magers, who has guarded the Ziglar name and reputation for forty-one years and makes me look good. Krish Dhanam for all of his wit, wisdom, and loyalty to our family for more than two decades, and for giving me the first working title of the book—*Live to Win*—which became *Choose to Win*. Bryan Flanagan, for being my coach on many occasions and having the knack of saying the right thing at the right time. Mark Timm, for having a huge vision of new ways for Ziglar to reach more people and helping me step into that.

ACKNOWLEDGMENTS

Kevin Miller, the host of *The Ziglar Show* who challenges me to think deeply and does a fantastic job curating the Ziglar message to the podcast world. Charles Ho, John Rouse, and Tyson Murphy, who have each walked deeply in the *Choose to Win* approach and helped me grow in the process. My mentors whom I get to call my friends and my supporters of the Ziglar mission and me: Seth Godin, Rabbi Daniel Lapin, Steve McKnight, Dave Ramsey, and Bob Tiede. Dale Dodson, who was there when I needed him most. DeWayne Owens, who prays for me all of the time. Brian Hampton and Jenny Baumgartner and their work at Thomas Nelson for making this book a reality. Most of all I want to acknowledge my Lord and Savior, Jesus Christ. I have seen too many miracles not to believe. I pray this book honors the Name above all Names.

NOTES

Chapter 3: Goals
1. Bob Beaudine, *2 Chairs* (Franklin, TN: Worthy, 2016).

Chapter 4: Desire, Hope, and Grit
1. *American Dictionary of the English Language* Online, 1828 edition, s.v. "desire," http://webstersdictionary1828.com/Dictionary/desire.
2. Angela Duckworth, *Grit* (NY: Simon & Shuster, 2016).

Chapter 6: Spiritual
1. Daniel Lapin, *Rabbi Daniel Lapin Podcast*, rabbidaniellapin.com /podcast.
2. Seth Godin, *Seth's blog* (blog), https://seths.blog/.
3. Robert Waldinger, "What Makes a Good Life? Lessons from the Longest Study on Happiness," TEDx, November 2015,https://www.ted.com/talks /robert_waldinger_what_makes_a_good_life_lessons_from_the _longest_study_on_happiness.
4. *American Dictionary of the English Language* Online, 1828 edition, s.v. "integrity," http://webstersdictionary1828.com/Dictionary/integrity.

Chapter 7: Physical
1. https://ziglarshow.com/.

Chapter 9: Financial
1. Rabbi Lapin, *Rabbi Daniel Lapin Podcast*, rabbidaniellapin.com /podcast.

Chapter 10: Personal

1. Bob Beaudine, *The Power of Who* (Center Street, 2009).
2. Laura F. Friedman and Kevin Loria, "11 Scientific Reasons You Should Be Spending More Time Outdoors," *Business Insider*, April 22, 2016, http://www.businessinsider.com/scientific-benefits-of-nature-outdoors-2016-4/#1-improved-short-term-memory-1.
3. Karen Ann Moore, *What a Great Word* (FaithWords, 2018).

Chapter 11: Career

1. Beaudine, *The Power of Who*.

ABOUT THE AUTHOR

Tom Ziglar is the proud son of Zig Ziglar and the CEO of Ziglar, Inc. He joined the Zig Ziglar Corporation in 1987 and climbed from working in the warehouse to sales, to management, and then on to leadership. Today, he speaks around the world; hosts *The Ziglar Show*, one of the top-ranked business podcasts; and carries on the Ziglar philosophy: "You can have everything in life you want if you will just help enough other people get what they want." He and his wife, Chachis, have one daughter and reside in Plano, Texas.